The Bookhams

in

World War II

Editors:

Peter G Clarke, Martin Warwick

Contributors:

Michael Anderson, John Chadwick, Hilary Chittenden, Peter G Clarke, Peter Crook, Barry Draper, Geoff Havers, Roy Mellick, Chris Pullan, Graham Wilson, Martin Warwick

Published by:

Leatherhead & District Local History Society

Printed by:
Surrey Litho Limited
Holders of The Royal Warrant to HRH The Prince of Wales as Designers and Printers

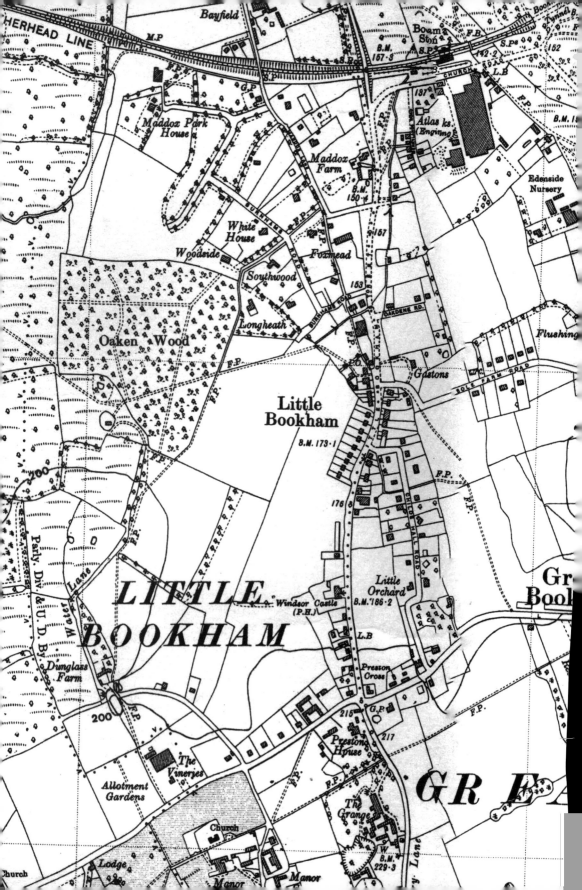

Acknowledgements and Thanks

Surrey History Centre, Woking

Leatherhead & District Local History Society

Leatherhead Advertiser (Greta Morley)

Contributors of Material

Publications

'Life Begins at Eighty', Dorothy Joce

'Turville', Wendy Young. Printed by BTF, Suffolk House, 1 Park Road, Hackbridge, Surrey, SM6 7ER (ISBN 09 534108 0 3)

'Bookham in the Twentieth Century', Bill Culley. Printed by JW Arrowsmith, Bristol (ISBN 0 9506009 7 0) (with the support of the Leatherhead & District Local History Society)

'Punch Goes to War' printed by Prius (2010) Carlton Publishing Group, 20 Mortimer Street, London W1T 3JW (ISBN 978 1 85375 769 3)

Royal Canadian Artillery

Par La Bouche De Nos Canons by Jacques Gouin

History of the 4th Medium Regt RCA 1941 -1945

Royal Canadian Engineers

Young Street - The Canadian Army at War

'The Canadians in Britain 1939 - 1944' Published by Authority of the Minister of National Defence

Regimental History of 3rd Field Survey Coy, RCE

Extracts from Diary of 4th Field Survey Coy, RCE

Interviewees

Rosemary Batchelor, Liz Finucane, Mary Fournier, John Gray, Geoff Griffiths, Dave Holland, David Hutton, Jim Kearney, Jill and Roger Lovegrove, Jessica and Tony Page, Richard Pankhurst, Roy Pitcher, Ken Poulter, Christopher Slater, Angela and John Stevens, Don White, Grace Williams

By Telephone

Peter Adams, Mary Eamus, Peggy Hester, Turville Kille (Jnr), Frank Reid, Barbara Smith.

Written Reminiscences

Pat Mace (Casselden), Tony Page, Joy Real (Martin), Jane Rose (Lovegrove), Kath Shepherd

Thanks are also due to Adele Couchman, Martin Francis, Ali Kelman, Terry Staff, Peter Tilley and Bill Whitman for their assistance.

Introduction

This book has been prepared by members of the Military History Group of the Bookham and District University of the Third Age (U3A) which itself is a member of the national U3A movement originally created to enable people no longer in full-time employment to continue with educational, creative, and learning opportunities in their daily lives.

It was realised by the Group in September 2010 that there was no consolidated record of events in the Bookhams during the second world war and the number of people with personal memories of this period was rapidly decreasing.

It was therefore decided to rectify this omission by producing a permanent record of wartime life in the villages. This was achieved by locating as much written and photographic material as possible and interviewing people who were living in or who came to the Bookhams in the War Years. Several Group members willingly volunteered to undertake these tasks and their efforts and findings form the basis of the book.

Our contributors made frequent visits to The Surrey History Centre in Woking and to the archives held by the Leatherhead History Society. They read through wartime copies of the Leatherhead Advertiser and Surrey Advertiser. The Bookhams Bulletin issues were also a rich source of information as were church magazines. These captured well the mood and happenings in the locality at that time.

Some material of a national nature has been introduced to set the scene as many younger readers will have little or no knowledge or experience of how wartime conditions affected the country as a whole.

The book describes how the nation and local inhabitants prepared for the conflict and how the area responded to evacuees from London on the outbreak of war.

Although on the fringes of the intense aerial bombardment in London in 1940/41, the villages experienced a number of attacks some of which were a result, generally believed, of German aircraft jettisoning their remaining bombs during their return to France. This period is graphically described in the extracts from a schoolboy's diary compiled at the time.

1944/45 saw the arrival of the V1 and V2 unmanned weapons with many flights of the former being experienced by people in the villages.

Life went on much as before the war with community activities continuing relatively unaffected except that food, materials and fuel rationing made life very difficult. With the addition of clothes rationing it was definitely a 'make do and mend' period.

A significant reminder that the war had really come to the Bookhams was the arrival in 1942 of the Canadian Army which in various ways contributed to the spirit of the community until the end of the war in August 1945.

Local celebrations marking the end of hostilities are well recorded and although the Bookhams largely escaped aerial attacks the book demonstrates that local people amply played their part in achieving victory by their individual and collective sacrifices. Details of those members of our communities who made the supreme sacrifice have been researched and recorded.

Our research has been fascinating and it is hoped that what has been written may help capture some of the local flavour of the times which would otherwise no longer be remembered.

John Chadwick
Group Leader
Military History Group
Bookham & District U3A

CON TENTS

Chapter 1

PRE-WAR BOOKHAM

THE 1930s

In the 1930s Great and Little Bookham were rural villages with a population of around four thousand compared with nearly twelve thousand today. A visitor would have viewed the area as a few small shops, businesses and scattered development together with small farms and smallholdings. There was a good rail service from Bookham Station to London but although commuting by rail was increasing the employment of the village remained essentially agricultural and the journey to work was likely to be a short distance for many residents. In addition there were businesses to serve local needs for example blacksmiths, dairies and services such as dressmaking and cobbling.

By the 1930s there were no 'Lords of the Manor' and the large manor houses such as Eastwick had been acquired for other use or had fallen out of use. There was the beginning of some development of council houses in Little Bookham Street and Fairfield Cottages but it was well before the time of the large spread housing and estates of today. The only very large mansion maintained in any splendour was Polesden Lacey under the charge of Mrs Greville.

HMV gramophones played fragile 78 rpm shellac records and their springs had to be wound up by hand and the volume controlled by opening the doors at the front. Many radio (often called wireless) sets were battery-operated and some were crystal sets which had to be listened to through headphones. However, more affluent households with mains electricity could take advantage of the availability of mains-powered radios or radiograms which could also play records. There was an extremely limited choice of programmes but possession of a reasonable set was the cause of friends getting together to listen to their favourite programmes. Television was in its infancy in 1939. The picture shows a relatively expensive Philco set which had a 6 inch screen and would have cost about £40 or in today's money £4,000. It is unlikely that there were any sets in Bookham at that time due to its distance from London's Alexandra Palace. The television service was completely closed down during the war and in

HMV Gramophone

Prewar Philco television with its 6 inch screen

The Duke and Duchess of York on their honeymoon at Polesden Lacey in 1923

general people made their own entertainment. An example of this was the local celebration to mark the 12th May 1937 coronation of King George VI and Queen Elizabeth at Westminster Abbey. The large number of events included a relay in Bookham's churches and recreation ground of the wireless broadcast commentary of the coronation procession and the service at the Abbey. Tea was provided for all the village children and supper and entertainment for the 'Old Folks' (over 65s). The day ended with a carnival dance and bonfire. The programme for this special day recalled the close association with the King who as the Duke of York had patronised the July 1922 'Great Fête' in Great Bookham and also that the Duke and Duchess had come to St Nicolas Church during the time they had spent at Polesden Lacey on their honeymoon in April 1923. The coronation festivities and other social activities in 1937 reflected the nature of a close-knit community.

POPULATION

In 1941 a total of 4,075 residents lived in the two villages compared with 3,465 residents in the 1931 census, which itself was almost double that of the 1921 census. The population was still low when compared with that of today with nearly 12,000 residents.

MONEY

Throughout this book reference is made to amounts of money and it is necessary to understand its value in the 1930s. It is difficult to have a direct multiplier as conditions were so different. In 2012 there is a minimum wage of something just over six pounds an hour which for a 40 hour week gives £240 a week or about £12,500 a year. In the 1930s the working week was far longer, 50 hours plus and Saturday was a working day or perhaps half day.

In the 1930s £100 a year was a workable family wage while a girl in service might get less than £50 a year. A person earning £500 per year was rich and £1,000 annually was a fortune. Working on this basis a reasonable multiplier to prices and values might be between one and two hundred. An example of this is the price of a small car (Austin 7, Morris 8, Ford 8) which was about £120 and £200 for a luxury version (if one of those cars could provide luxury). A reasonable house could be bought for between one and two thousand pounds.

The prewar Austin 7 Ruby

There were different monetary denominations then. In the 'old money' there were 240 pence to the pound and a farthing was a quarter of a penny. Today sums of money are written using a decimal point such as £12.50 but then money was in pounds, shillings and pence (£sd or LSD) and you might see an amount of £2 13s 5¼d. In those days a farthing was really worth something and could buy a packet of sweets. Ten shillings was usually written as 10/- and 2s 9d as 2/9.

'Old Money' showing a one pound note, a florin (two shillings), a sixpenny bit, a penny and a threepenny bit

HOUSING

During the inter-war period the character of the Bookhams was changing. Up to that time the number of large estates with substantial houses and powerful owners had provided work for many local people. However whilst there was still a large involvement in agriculture with a short journey to work, commuting to London was increasingly reflected in the growth in population at that time. Businesses developed to serve local needs for example blacksmiths, dairies and services such as dressmaking and cobbling.

There was not the same accent placed on owning a house in the 1930s as today and most ordinary houses were rented. Very often the 'rent collector' would call once a week to collect the rent which might vary from 10s 6d to 15s 6d per week.

The condition of the smaller village houses was inspected regularly by the council to ensure that

An outdoor 'loo'

there was no overcrowding and that sanitary conditions were satisfactory. Most of those to which reference was made in reports were two-up/two-down in size and all those checked at least had running water, referred to as 'Town Water'. Electricity supplies in the home were not commonplace and even at the Little Bookham Church Rectory electricity was not installed until a year after the war, at a total cost of £140. Houses were often lit by gas using gas lights with a 'mantle' or even by candlelight.

All houses in the central area had a WC (water closet) but those in outlying areas had only 'Pail Closets'. Farm cottages had sink drains discharging into adjacent fields. Each house had a dustbin. Dampness was clearly a problem and many inspections resulted in instructions to deal with such matters as defective window frames, leaking roofs and frequently to strip and replace wallpaper.

These inspection reports were not restricted to housing but relevant to the more rural nature of the community. One in November 1938 on the local cowsheds records the following:

Bookham Grove: 10 cows. Milk sold to the public in their own receptacles

Slyfield Farm: 100 cows, in good state

The Grange: 5 cows

Bookham High Street shortly after the war

*Prewar aerial view of the crossing of Lower Road, Crabtree Lane and Eastwick Road. Gau &
Lawes (now Hylands) Garage can be seen. Note the low density of the housing.*

LOCAL BUSINESSES

Once the war commenced, it is clear that the shopkeepers were under considerable pressure dealing
with rationing, shortages in food supplies (often as a result of enemy action affecting their suppliers)
and the impact of supplying evacuees.

It is apparent that the number of retail outlets changed little during the war years and in fact numbers
remain similar even to this day. It is merely the character of the shops that has changed for example
supermarkets replacing general stores. Great Bookham remains almost unique in retaining specialist
shops such as butchers, a bakery and a fishmonger. Bookham had a Co-op for many years – albeit
in a different location. The village streets in some ways retain much of the atmosphere of bygone
years making shopping a less stressful experience than elsewhere.

The four public houses seen today were open for business in the war years – namely The Windsor
Castle in Little Bookham, and in Great Bookham, The Anchor, The Royal Oak and The Old Crown,
the latter having been rebuilt only in 1932.

During the war years there was a considerable reliance on all the local retail shops. Appendix A
contains a 1939 list of Bookham retail shops, their names, their businesses and addresses.

The Garage of W Armstrong & Sons in Lower Road (now T W White & Sons) which was later owned by Ken Barrington, the England cricketer. Church House was adjacent to it on the left.

THE LARGER HOUSES

Prior to the breakout of war in 1939 the larger houses and their estates had a major influence on the lives of the people living in the two villages.

Polesden Lacey

Polesden Lacey was owned by the Hon Mrs Ronald Greville, the well known Edwardian society hostess. The house and estate provided a considerable amount of local employment right up to the beginning of the war. The total of her staff numbered some 70 divided between Polesden Lacey and her London house with many travelling with her as she moved between the residences. They included butlers, footmen, coachmen, manservants, maids and gardeners, some of whom lived in tied cottages, flats and attics in the house as well as locally in the villages.

At the outbreak of war Mrs Greville was 76 and was permanently living in London but not at her private residence, 16 Charles St, Mayfair but at the Dorchester Hotel. On Mrs Greville's death in 1942 Polesden Lacey house, art collections and extensive estate were left to the National Trust. Amongst her other bequests she left all her jewellery to Queen Elizabeth which is currently in the Royal Collection and £20,000 (a considerable sum in those days) to Princess Margaret.

During the war Polesden Lacey was used to store various articles including papers but safety and security reasons at the time prevent us knowing the exact details. There were some officers, probably British, stationed there at some time because there was a sentry at the drive entrance. There is a

*Polesden
Lacey House*

reference to an official, James Lees-Milne, visiting the house during the war and assessing the collection of papers that had been moved there.

There is some doubt as to exactly how else Polesden Lacey house was utilised in wartime. It is known however that the Royal Army Service Corps had a presence at least in the woods on the estate. The St Nicolas Parish Magazine also records that personnel from that Corps attended church services.

Eastwick Park

Eastwick Park, originally the seat of the Howard family, was no longer retained as a Manor House after the First World War and had been leased as a school in 1924. The school was named Southey Hall Boys' Preparatory School as it had been transferred from Southey Road in Worthing with the consequence that the old Eastwick Park became known as Southey Hall. By the beginning of the war there were sixty to seventy boarders in addition to day boys. The house was vacated by the school in 1954 and was later demolished.

Bookham Grove House

Bookham Grove House (built some time before 1720 and originally the seat of the Dawnay family) was in private ownership at the start of the war and remained so up to 1956 when the property was divided into flats.

Bayfield (Bookham Grange Hotel)

Bayfield, originally a farmhouse was in the 1930's a nursing home until it was found to be 'conducting illegal operations at the premises'. In the war years, it was occupied by the Imperial Bank of India when it evacuated its London offices.

Preston House

Preston House was a private residence and remained so until 1970 when it became Preston Cross Hotel. During the war it was used by the Women's Voluntary Service for the production of clothing.

Eastwick Park House, later known as Southey Hall

Rear view of Bookham Grove House

Bayfield, later the Bookham Grange Hotel, previously a nursing home.

The Grange in Rectory Lane later the School of Stitchery and Lace

A workroom in the School of Stitchery and Lace at the Grange

The Old Rectory in Rectory Lane originally the Rectory to Little Bookham Church

The Old Rectory to St Nicolas Church in Church Road now no longer there

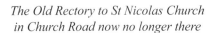

Victoria Hotel now Rayleigh House with a view down the High Street prior to the straightening of the Leatherhead - Guildford Road

Millfield on the Cobham Road now part of The Yehudi Menuhin School of Music

The Grange

The house in Rectory Lane had previously been the residence of Arthur Bird, a considerable landowner in Bookham who gave the Old Barn Hall to the parish. Just before the war in 1938 the School of Stitchery and Lace was established there with the aim of 'training disabled people in needlework skills as well as providing sheltered workshops and accommodation'.

The Old Rectory in Rectory Lane

In Rectory Lane the Old Rectory functioned as a rectory until 1900, but in wartime and until 1947, was occupied by Queen Maria of Yugoslavia, widow of King Alexander I who had been assassinated in Marseille in 1934. Her mother was Queen Marie of Romania, a daughter of Prince Alfred, Duke of Edinburgh, son of Queen Victoria. Her son was King Peter II, the last King of Yugoslavia. She is stated to have lived here 'without royal extravagance and even drove her own car'. She died in London in 1961 (aged 61) and was interred at Frogmore, Windsor.

The Old Rectory in Church Road

This Old Rectory was the rectory to St Nicolas Church built in the late 18th century. It stood behind the current parade of shops in Church Road . The house was demolished in 1961 after being empty since the 1930s. Jane Austen visited her godfather, the Vicar, Samuel Cooke here in 1809 and 1814.

Victoria Hotel

The Victoria Hotel now known as Rayleigh House at the junction of the High Street and Guildford Road had been built as a Temperance Hotel in the first instance by Mrs Chrystie, an ardent temperance worker and supporter of the Band of Hope. During the war and up to 1943 it was used as Home Guard Headquarters, the British Restaurant and ARP Centre after which it was used to house Canadian troops.

Millfield

On the Cobham Road this large house during the War was used as offices and a military establishment. It is now incorporated in the Yehudi Menuhin School of Music.

INDUSTRY

As is the case today, industrial businesses were few and far between in the Bookham villages in the War years. Nevertheless, the only factory of any size made a significant contribution to the national war effort.

Gillett Stephen

In the early 1900s Thomas Gillett opened a general engineering works in Little Bookham Street in the original Atlas Works extending to about 2,000 square feet. The business was incorporated as Gillett Stephen and Company Ltd in 1912 and during the First World War the whole capacity was turned over to wartime production. Aircraft parts were manufactured, including components for radial engines for the Royal Aircraft Establishment at Farnborough. This original building was

Top: Gillett Stephen New Atlas works. At the bottom left hand corner is Bookham Station - note the railway sidings stretching to the front of the factory

Bottom: The old Atlas Works in Little Bookham Street next to Vine Cottage

A scene of the factory floor

Some of the undercarriage parts made in the factory

demolished in 1968 to be replaced by the Blackburn flats.

The engineering business was expanding and Thomas Gillett in partnership with a Mr Waring of the Waring & Gillow firm following the death of Mrs Mary Chrystie acquired the Merrylands Hotel opposite the Railway Station to convert to offices and to build an additional factory in the grounds. The Merrylands Hotel had originally been established as a Temperance Hotel in 1885. The factory was known as the New Atlas Works which expanded in stages giving a total of about 120,000 square feet of workspace between the two sites by the time of the First World War, sixty times the size of the original workshop.

Burney & Blackburne also occupied premises at the Atlas Works' sites. They were a very well known company and their proprietary Blackburne engines were used in a variety of airplanes, cars (including racing cars), motor cycles and even motor torpedo boats and agricultural machinery in the period between the two world wars. These proprietary engines were used by about a dozen aircraft manufacturers, around eighty to ninety motor cycle makers and thirty car makers making Gillett Stephen an engine maker of some repute. The range of small light aircraft engines included the Tomtit and the Thrush.

By 1934 Gillett Stephen was already manufacturing aircraft undercarriages and hydraulic equipment and, when rearmament commenced in 1936, the company received a large contract not only for undercarriages but also for the manufacture of incendiary bombs. With the increasing emphasis on the manufacture of undercarriages and hydraulic parts as war approached, the manufacture of Blackburne engines ceased never to start again.

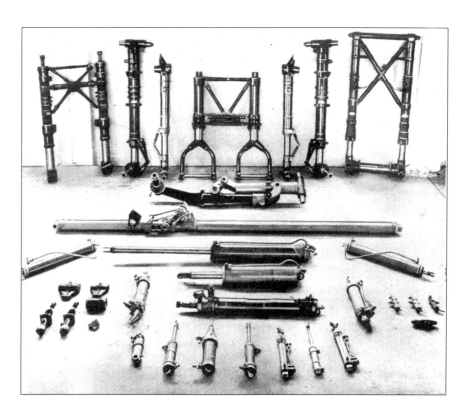

A further selection of some of the Gillett Stephen aircraft parts made during the war

The factory was extremely busy in the war years with the production of parts for many aircraft including the Airspeed Oxford, Avro Anson, Lancaster and Manchester, Bristol Beaufighter, de Havilland Flamingo and Mosquito, Handley Page Halifax and Hampden, Hawker Hurricane, Tornado, Typhoon and Tempest, Short Stirling, Vickers Armstrong Supermarine Spitfire and Westland Whirlwind. It is also understood that Gillett Stephen were the sole manufacturers of undercarriages fitted to both the Hawker Typhoons and Handley Page Hampdens. The company was highly regarded as a specialist firm in the manufacture of undercarriages with considerable experience with dealing with the problems associated with this type of equipment. Each of the 3,333 Hawker Typhoon and the 1,453 Handley Page Hampden aircraft produced had an undercarriage made by Gillett Stephen, and it was calculated in 1944 that up to then 100,000 aircraft hydraulic assemblies had been made in this factory.

It would appear that intelligence of their essential and important work was not recognised by the Germans as the factory was not bombed.

The Mill in Church Road

The mill originally constructed as a steam powered corn mill in 1830 was adapted in about 1913 to be a sawmill. During the war years it processed wood for railway wagons, railway sleepers, temporary landing slips etc. Another activity which took place there was the filling of palliasses with straw for use by the army.

The Mill in Church Road

Chapter 2

PREPARATIONS FOR WAR

1917 had seen the Bolshevik uprising in Russia. Following the Wall Street Stock Market collapse in America in 1929 the Great Depression devastated Europe causing widespread poverty with millions out of work. Even in England Fascist marches took place under Oswald Moseley. Hitler took advantage of the unrest by coming to power in Germany in 1934. General Franco came to power in Spain and Mussolini in Italy. The future aims of Hitler became apparent when in 1938 first Austria and later Czechoslovakia were absorbed into Germany . Every attempt was being made at diplomatic level to prevent a further war by a policy of appeasement under the government of the then prime minister Neville Chamberlain. Meanwhile Winston Churchill and others saw the inevitability of a further conflict and the urgent need to prepare for war.

CIVIL DEFENCE

It is surprising to realise the extent to which the Government had been preparing for war as far back as 1924 only six years after the end of the First World War. In that year it set up the Imperial Defence Committee, the forerunner of the Air Raid Precautions (ARP) under Sir John Anderson to examine the future implications of war with consideration of matters such as evacuation, gas masks and lighting restrictions. It was later in 1935 that Stanley Baldwin published a circular inviting local authorities to take measures to protect people in the event of a war. A few authorities complied but others did not!

MILITARY SERVICE - CONSCRIPTION

In 1937 there were 200,000 soldiers in the British army. The government knew that this was not enough to fight a war with Germany and in April 1939 introduced the National Service (Armed Forces) Act by which most fit men of military age in the UK (normally between the ages of 18 and 41) were conscripted into the Armed Forces. By 1942 however all fit males who were British residents – as well as unmarried females aged between 20 and 30 years - were liable to be called up. At the beginning of the War, the wage of a Private in the Army was 2s per day (10p in today's money or £36.50 per year) whilst a Sergeant earned 7s per day (35p or £127.75 per year). In contrast, a Land Girl was paid £1 8s per week or £72.80 a year.

In 1938, however, a Schedule of Reserved Occupations was drawn up exempting certain key skilled workers from conscription (initially five million in the UK as a whole). A Reserved Occupation was one that was considered vital to the country or the war effort and which could not be abandoned or performed by others. This schedule was subsequently regularly reviewed during the War years particularly as more women were steadily being taken into the workforce who could then take on certain roles, thereby freeing some men to be called up into the Armed Forces. When compiling this Schedule the Government clearly had in mind the situation which arose in the First World War at which time too many men were taken into the Armed Forces leaving major war production schemes short of a workforce. Many of the men in Reserved Occupations also joined Civil Defence units such as the Special Constabulary, the Home Guard and the ARP.

It is likely that in an area such as the Bookham villages, the Reserved Occupations would have included farmers, agricultural workers, schoolteachers, doctors and some who were employed in various forms of engineering.

Under the National Service (Armed Forces) Act 1939, Conscientious Objectors (individuals claiming the right to refuse to perform military service on the grounds of freedom of thought, conscience and/or religion) could submit a claim for exemption and would have to go before a tribunal. It appears that nationally out of a total of 60,000 such claimants only 3,000 were granted complete exemption.

AIR RAID WARDENS AND AIR RAID PRECAUTIONS (ARP)

The Government decided in April 1937 to set up the Air Raid Wardens Service and had recruited around 200,000 volunteers by November 1938. A public meeting was arranged in January 1937 by Leatherhead Urban District Council (LUDC) to discuss air raid procedures and it was emphasised that such procedures must be set in motion without delay. Volunteers were invited for roles including: Wardens, First Aid, Demolition and Fire Fighting.

There was growing concern about the various forms of attack which might ensue, for example the use of gas or germ warfare. Commencing in October 1937 a series of six lectures on 'Anti-Gas measures' was given at the Old Barn Hall. In February 1938 ARP training started for Wardens and comment was made that the enrolment of Wardens was going well locally. In fact by May 1938 Bookham had sixty eight ARP Wardens of whom fifty four were stated to have been trained.

By March 1939 all residents had been issued with the 'National Service Book', a booklet entitled 'The protection of your home against air raids' and a pamphlet: 'Transfer of population in times of war'. In the following months, before the actual declaration of war in September, various leaflets were issued and distributed to everyone including those entitled: 'Some things you should know if war comes', 'Air

Raid Warnings', 'Gas Masks', 'Lighting Restrictions', 'Fire Precautions', 'Evacuation' 'Identity Labels', 'Food' and 'Instructions to the public in case of emergency'. The location of five ARP posts in Bookham had been announced.

A Home Defence Exercise was arranged for August 1939 for every Local Authority in the County. It was expected that all households should blackout their premises between 11.55pm. and 4.00am. The BBC broadcast messages to say that people should put up blackout curtains not just go to bed without putting on lights.

THE BOOKHAMS.

FIRE GUARD SCHEME. — A representative meeting of local Fire Guards was held in the Village Hall, Little Bookham, on Friday last, when the Chief Warden of the Leatherhead Urban District Council (Mr. John T. Probert) spoke on the "functions and control of the incendiary bomb." He was supported by Capt. James Douglas (Divisional Warden), Mr. T. E. Etlinger (Deputy Divisional Warden and Head Fire Guard), Mr. C. V. Brayne (Head Warden) and Mr. E. Brett (Fire Party Leader). A practical demonstration in fire fighting and the use of the stirrup pump was given by Mrs. D. I. Bentley, of the Bookham Wardens' Service.

The Chief ARP Warden of the LUDC was a Mr J.T.Probert. The wardens

Gillett Stephen had their own air raid and fire teams

worked a minimum of twelve hours per week. The number was apparently higher than the Government required and it appears that a number of wardens had to resign and become Fire Guards whose duty was to look after the Bookham shopping area. The Fire Guard for the High Street was Mr F E Allman, for Church Road, Messrs Mills Bros and for the Leatherhead Road, Mr W L Coles,

ARP Badge and 'Tin Hat'

Mr E C Ovens and Mr E Barford. Gillett Stephen whose factory was opposite Bookham Station had its own ARP and AFS teams. Among other locations there were Wardens' Posts at Flushing Farm, 'Malvern' in Leatherhead Road and the junction of Dorking Road and Dowlans Road.

These were among the moves designed to prepare the local population for war in the period leading up to the actual declaration of War in September 1939.

STIRRUP PUMPS

One hundred and nine stirrup pumps were recorded as being available in Bookham in January 1941. They were issued to fire watchers and fire guards to put out fires resulting from incendiary bombs or other bombing.

A Stirrup Pump

"Splendid! Splendid! You've ALMOST got the hang of it."

(cartoon from 'Punch goes to War 1939-1945')

AIR RAID SIRENS

One air raid siren in Bookham was originally situated outside The Old Crown, although it was later moved to a site adjoining the Church Hall in Lower Road where Church House now stands. A further siren was located at the Atlas Works of Gillet Stephen. The sirens were sounded when German aircraft came within thirty miles of Bookham. It was an almost

An Air Raid Siren

constant feature of local life during The Battle of Britain and The Blitz. One local resident who kept a daily diary at that time recorded ninety five alerts in the five weeks from 13th August to 19th September 1940 (see Appendix B). It also sounded frequently when the V1 Flying Bombs and the V2 rockets arrived.

SEARCHLIGHTS & BARRAGE BALLOONS

There was a searchlight positioned near Bocketts Farm as well as others in the area. There was also a barrage balloon in the field by the turn from Dorking Road to Polesden Lacey. Triangular pits on the Eastern Plain (just north of the Tunnel Car Park) of Bookham Common once had a concrete base and an anti-aircraft gun on them.

A Barrage Balloon and Searchlight. The Barrage Balloons were inflated with Hydrogen

GAS MASKS

There was a very real fear in Britain that German bombers would drop poison gas bombs and all civilians were therefore issued with gas masks. The government had forecast tens of thousands of deaths in London alone. An advisor to the government, Liddell Hart, told the government to expect a quarter of a million deaths in the first week of the war alone. Nationally, by December 1938, three million gas masks had already been issued. It was the responsibility of air raid wardens to ensure that everybody had been issued with a gas mask and the public were encouraged to report any omissions. Advice from the Leatherhead Urban District Council in the early stages of the war was that gas masks should be worn for an hour each day as a practice, even when answering the telephone!

Special gas masks were made for babies but were only to be issued if an emergency situation arose. Children were issued with what became known as 'Mickey Mouse' gas masks - the nickname was an attempt by the government to make the gas masks seem less scary.

Hitler will send no warning – so always carry your gas mask

ISSUED BY THE MINISTRY OF HOME SECURITY

A standard gas mask with several filters for different gases. Wearing while telephoning had its difficulties even in practice!

Gas Masks for Babies with the 'Mickey Mouse' model

The Ministry of Home Safety issued advice on how to put on a gas mask:

> Hold your breath
>
> Hold mask in front of face with thumbs inside straps
>
> Thrust chin well forward into mask, pull straps over head as far as they will go
>
> Run finger round face piece taking care head straps are not twisted
>
> If out of doors people were advised to turn up their jacket collar to stop gas drifting down necks and to put on gloves or put hands in pockets to stop gas getting to skin

An anti-gas course was held in the Red Cross Hall in Leatherhead and organised by James Douglas, Divisional Warden of Great Bookham on 29th July 1939.

After the Blitz had ended, carrying around a gas mask became less and less important in the mind of the public.

AUXILIARY FIRE SERVICE (AFS)

Neville Chamberlain had mobilised the ARP a year earlier in 1938 and put Sir John Anderson in charge. At the same time the Government directed local authorities to recruit and train auxiliary firemen for the Auxiliary Fire Service (AFS) who became part of their local fire brigade. The LUDC which covered the Bookhams, Ashtead, Fetcham and Leatherhead recruited men from these areas and at the beginning of the war substations were set up.

The Section Leader in charge in Bookham was Turville Kille with seventeen crew men. They were split into three crews, and four would be on duty once every three nights. Their station by Gau &

Back Row: Les Ebsworth, Harry Absalom, A N Other, George (Joe) Shepherd, Bob Rye, Alf Wesley, Tom Noble, Bill Edwards, Elmer Absalom
Front Row: Ronnie Lambert, Hugh Fortescue, Turville Kille, Jack Sharp

Left to Right: A N Other, Joe Shepherd, Hugh Fortescue, Ronnie Lambert and Turville Kille

Lawes (now Highlands Garage) was equipped with a Ford V8 car which was used to tow a trailer-pump and to carry the extension ladder. There are various anecdotes in the book 'The Life and Times of Turville Kille' and the photographs and cartoon below are taken from that book. The cartoon recaptures the celebrated occasion when the trailer overturned on the bend going down Church Road towards the railway station throwing off two policemen who were, unknown to the fire crew, hitching a lift.

Because the large number of independent fire brigades needed some form of overall co-ordination the National Fire Service was formed in 1941 and control was removed from the local authorities.

The cartoon of one of the AFS's somewhat hasty responses to a fire

ARP FOR ANIMALS

A National ARP for Animals Committee was formed for the area with a Bookham representative appointed to find volunteers to act as 'Animal Guards'. These for example would provide for the prevention and alleviation of suffering, protect humans from panic stricken animals, the conservation of animals of economic value and the protection and provision of food supplies for essential animals.

RED CROSS

The Red Cross headquarters was based at the Old Barn Hall but a first aid post also operated out of Church House, Lower Road along with the ARP.

2nd World War : Key to Group Photograph, vol 1 p.134- Surrey 26 Red Cross Detachment. Barn Hall, Great Bookham. (Left to Right).

Back Row : Mrs Freelove, —, Mrs Phillips, Mrs Tatham, Mrs Waterfield, Mrs Cruickshank, Dorothy Longley, Gillian Brown (daughter of the Commandant), Mrs Aver, Mrs Muir-Simpson, Mrs May Dibdin, Miss Crawley?, Mrs Eade, Mrs Loxley.

Middle Row : Miss Elsie Micholls Mrs Nesta McGowan, Mrs Champion, Mrs Marion Floud (wife of the Vicar af Effingham), Mrs 'Da' Perry, Dr Noel Waterfield, Mrs Gerda L. Brown (Commandant, who set up the fully equipped First Aid Post and formed the Detachment), Mrs Buckley, Mrs Crumplin, Lady Mallaby Deeley, —, Mrs Hart.

Front Row : —, Miss Shaw, Miss Haviland, Mrs George, Miss Shoosmith, Miss Maud Micholls, —, Mrs Martin, — .

Surrey 26th Red Cross Detachment outside the old Church House

WOMEN'S LAND ARMY (WLA)

The Women's Land Army which was founded in the First World War was reformed in 1942, but very little information now seems to be available about the WLA in Bookham. The WLA Surrey County Committee was based at the educational office in Park Street in Guildford. The only mention found was 'Other incomers on the local farms were members of the Women's Land Army with their bright green sweaters and buff coloured jodhpurs who were based at Epsom'.

BLACKOUT REGULATIONS

The blackout regulations stipulated that no light must be seen from the outside of the home between the hours of 11.55pm and 4.00am and therefore windows, glazed doors and other openings had to be completely covered by thick curtains (or blinds of stout material and of a dark colour).

An official reminder was issued in December 1940 that 'torches used during an Alert must be dimmed with a piece of newspaper or its equivalent, the aperture must be not more than one inch (the diameter of a halfpenny) and they must be directed downwards'.

All the churches reacted to regulations at least in the early years of the war by moving their evening services to the afternoons. The Rector of St Nicolas commented "I know that the time is an inconvenient one but there is no alternative. It has become a point of honour with us as a nation to carry on our national life in spite of assault."

PUBLIC AIR RAID SHELTERS

The following quotation comes from the local Advertiser:

> 'It was estimated that the population of the Urban District (Leatherhead) was now 27,269, and to provide shelters to accommodate six per cent of the population who might be caught in the street, would require accommodation for 1,636. There was already accommodation for 490, leaving 1,246 to be provided for. He suggested these shelters should be of the brick pill-box type. To meet the population not now dealt with would require thirty two shelters, six each at Leatherhead and Fetcham, eleven at Ashtead, seven at Great Bookham, and two at Little Bookham. The estimated cost was £3,384.' (October 1940)

The location of one of the Bookham shelters is shown in the photograph. Another was by the Mixed School which was where the library now stands. Someone who was at school in Bookham in the war describes this shelter which had to be accessed by a flight of steps as being "long and narrow with slats of wood along each side for us to sit on and a small space in the middle to get from one end to the other. It was lit by one very dim central light bulb, so reading or having a lesson of any kind was impossible. I recall that all the children occupied the slats, and with the guidance of the teacher spent our time there singing. I recall that the shelter felt very cold and damp."

In March 1942 the LUDC ARP and National Defence Emergency Committee (which also covered Bookham) decided that public shelters would be kept locked during the day but unlocked during alerts and black-out times. The minutes of the meeting note that this did not deter certain of the military from forcing the doors and misusing the shelters!

This bump in the grass opposite The Paddocks off Guildford Road shows the location of a Public Air Raid Shelter from WWII

ANDERSON AND MORRISON SHELTERS

In November 1938, Chamberlain placed Sir John Anderson in charge of Air Raid Precautions (ARP). He immediately commissioned the engineer, William Patterson, to design a small and cheap shelter that could be erected in people's gardens. Within a few months nearly one and a half million of what became known as Anderson shelters were distributed to people living in areas expected to be bombed.

Made from six curved corrugated iron sheets bolted together at the top, with a steel plate at each end, and measuring 6ft 6in by 4ft 6in (1.95m by 1.35m) the shelter could accommodate six people. These shelters were half buried in the ground with earth heaped on top. The entrance was protected by a steel shield and an earthen blast wall.

Anderson shelters were provided free to low income families. Men who earned more than £5 a

An Anderson Shelter as they used to be dug into the garden

week could buy one for £7. Soon after the outbreak of war in September 1939 over two million families had shelters in their garden. By the time of the Blitz this had risen to two and a quarter million.

When the Luftwaffe changed from daylight to night bombing raids, the government expected people to sleep in their Anderson shelters. Each night the wailing of air raid sirens announced the approach of German bombers and ensured that people had time to take cover before the raid actually started.

Anderson shelters were dark and damp and people were reluctant to use them at night. In low-lying areas they tended to flood and sleeping was difficult as they did not keep out the sound of the bombing. Another problem was that the majority of people living in industrial areas did not have gardens where shelters could be erected.

A census in London held in November 1940 discovered that the majority of people there did not use specially created shelters. The London survey revealed that of those interviewed, 27% used Anderson shelters, 9% slept in public shelters whereas 4% used underground railway stations. The rest of those interviewed either slept in their own homes or were on duty at night.

In the second year of the war however the government began issuing Morrison Shelters. Named after the Home Secretary, Herbert Morrison, the shelters were made of very heavy steel and could be put in the living room and used as a table. One wire side lifted up for people to crawl underneath and get inside. Morrison shelters were fairly large and provided sleeping space for two or three people.

A Morrison Shelter inside the living room

Chapter 3

THE OUTBREAK OF WAR

The peaceful life that existed in the Bookham villages was to be shattered by the outbreak of war. The British declaration of war against Nazi Germany came at 11.15am on 3rd September 1939. The Prime Minister, Neville Chamberlain spoke to the nation via radio. Britain had given Hitler an ultimatum to withdraw from Poland after the Germans invaded Poland on 1st September.

"I am speaking to you from the Cabinet Room at 10, Downing Street. This morning the British Ambassador in Berlin handed the German Government a final note stating that unless we heard from them by 11.00am that they were prepared at once to withdraw their troops from Poland, a state of war would exist between us. I have to tell you that no such undertaking has been received, and that consequently this country is at war with Germany...........................

Now may God bless you all. May He defend the right. It is the evil things that we shall be fighting against – brute force, bad faith, injustice, oppression and persecution – and against them I am certain that the right will prevail."

If you had been at the 11 o'clock service in St Nicolas Church on that Sunday, 3rd September 1939 you would have seen the Churchwarden hand the Rector, Alec Hughes, a note which he then read out to advise the congregation of the declaration of war. It was written on a piece of scrap paper which has survived and is now held by the Surrey History Centre in Woking. It reads:

'Mr Chamberlain has just announced that, having had no reply from Germany, we are at war.'

On the reverse is a note from the Rector, initialled by him which reads:

'This note was handed to me during service on Sunday September 3rd. Read from the Pulpit.'

A tiny piece of paper bearing news which would severely disrupt the lives of every resident. The war had arrived in Bookham!

EVACUEES

Plans to evacuate mothers and young children and schools from London and other cities to safer locations had been in place for some years.

The wartime evacuation plans were code-named 'Operation Pied Piper'. This was an interesting choice when you think that in the original story only a handful at most of the youngsters who had been led out of the town by the Pied Piper actually returned to Hamelin!

The first Evacuees arrived in Bookham in late September 1939 - probably on Friday 22nd and Saturday 23rd. The first group, of teachers and small children, came by train at around 6.30 in the evening. A second from the Strand School in Tulse Hill, arrived at 11.30am the next day to be followed by a group of mothers and small children at 7.00 in the evening. Other evacuees arrived by bus.

MINISTRY OF HEALTH EVACUATION SCHEME

The mothers and children were taken up to Polesden Lacey where they were given 'a kindly, hospitable welcome' by Mrs Greville and her staff. The others who arrived by train were either taken by bus or walked in a crocodile from the station up to the Baptist Church Hall. In all probably some 500/600 children, mothers and teachers arrived in Bookham at that time. They were met at the Baptist Church Hall by Billeting Officers and local residents. The residents were there to choose which of the children they would take into their homes. It was a process which elsewhere was described as being like a 'cattle market'. Foster parents who were advertised for locally as in the advertisement on the left were paid 12/6d per child per week.

Thank you, Mrs. Ruggles···
we want more like you!

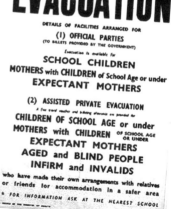

But it really was a traumatic time for those youngsters particularly those who had travelled without their mothers. These were town children who might well never ever have been out of town.

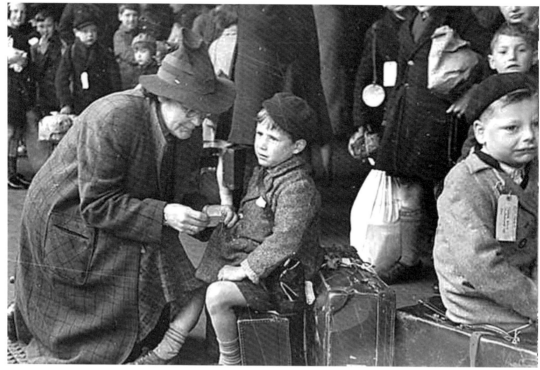

Evacuees waiting to be taken to their new homes

Pupils at the Dawnay School in the school play 'Evacuees' in 2011

Just arrived, neatly labelled and lined up waiting to be placed in foster homes

In the words of one of them, "You don't see country in London. All you see is roads .... we didn't see animals or nothing." The children would have woken the day after they had arrived living with people they did not know, in a strange house and in an unfamiliar environment. Many of them also experienced resentment from some of the local children ... "the village children were playing and they saw us and threw stones at us and told us Londoners to go back to London", or in the words of another evacuee "I was seen as a foreigner and roughed up by the local boys." Interestingly one evacuee had the same experience when he returned later to his home community - so maybe it was just a common reaction against strangers.

Some youngsters arrived with their schools (including those from the Strand School in Tulse Hill). They were soon settled in new premises and resumed their studies. Others were not so fortunate. With no full-time tuition in place they were kept occupied by, for example, being taken down to Bookham Common, boys and girls in separate groups. Some did not resume full-time education for months, although the Old Barn Hall was used for some to do homework in the afternoons. All the evacuees were given lunch at the Old Barn Hall.

Quite a few evacuees returned home in the early months of the war, however many came back to Bookham in the Blitz and later when the Doodlebugs began to arrive. Indeed in late 1942 the Bookham Billeting Officer lost his job because it was considered the arrangements for billeting fifty nine pupils from The Strand School had been bungled. Arrangements were not in fact published until August 1945 to cover the final return home of evacuees.

It is interesting that a number of evacuees remained living in Bookham after the war and that others came back to live here later.

CITIZENS' ADVICE BUREAU (CAB)

The Bookhams Citizens Advice Bureau opened in July 1939 and was the first of its kind in Surrey. The Bookhams Bulletin of December 1940 records that it had provided advice on many problems including billeting, war damage to property, the position of landlord and tenant in cases where destruction of property has occurred through bombing, and even obtaining employment for those who had lost their jobs on account of air raids. These matters and many others had all received immediate attention and resulted in a happier state of mind and lessening of anxiety.

HOME DEFENCE

The Local Defence Volunteers (LDV) was formed in May 1940 following Anthony Eden's speech in his role as Secretary of State for War, seeking male volunteers aged between 17 and 65 to join a force to defend the UK.

The Government had expected about 150 thousand men, but in the first 24 hours some 250 thousand men had volunteered and by the end of June, there were 1.5 million volunteers, approximately 40% of whom were experienced soldiers, mainly veterans from the First World War. The numbers never went below one million until they were disbanded.

Winston Churchill changed the name in July 1940 from

LDV to the Home Guard because he felt the original name was uninspiring. Perhaps the nickname of 'Look, Duck and Vanish' also had something to do with it!

When the Home Guard was first formed it had its own rank structure. From February 1941 the Army ranks were adopted for all ranks with the exception of privates who remained as volunteers until the spring of 1942 at which time they became privates. December 1941 saw the Government introduce the National Service Act No. 2 and all males from the age of 18 to 51 were liable to be called up for service in the Home Guard and from June 1943 women were allowed to serve.

Initially the LDV had no uniforms and wore 'LDV' armbands. At the start in Bookham, according to one local account they were armed with 'pikes, sticks and a farmer's confiscated shotgun'. Eventually they

HQ Platoon B Company 6th Battallion Home Guard

were issued with uniforms and rifles, mainly First World War American and Canadian weapons.

In September 1942 the Dorking Advertiser reported the following:

'After lectures and demonstrations by Lieut Brion of the Home Guard, The Bookham Platoon of the Army Cadet Force had their first experience of actual firing at the Home Guard miniature range in Bookham. All those who turned up were given five rounds each. Lieut Brion, a first class shot himself, was well satisfied with the results, and, as he said: "The accuracy of the shooting this time isn't so very important. What I want to see is a marked improvement next time." At the following parade he lectured the Cadets on ammunition, the various types and their uses. The Bookham Platoon under the command of Lieut D G Cook, attended the recent company parade. There was an inspection by Major C E Fox-Male, MC who, in a short address told the cadets of a sports day in the near future. Mr B Leat of the

Cutting from the Leatherhead Advertiser

THE BOOKHAMS.

HOME GUARD SHOOT.—Members of "B" Company, 6th Batt. Surrey Home Guard, had a shoot on Boxing Day. when prizes to the number of 50 were given by local residents and tradesmen of the Bookhams. These ranged from a load of farmyard manure to a dozen eggs. The winner was Corpl. E. C. Winter, with 2nd Lieut. E. W. Brion second. The prizes were presented by Major H. Teesdale, the Commanding Officer.

Effingham Platoon, Home Guard, is continuing his instruction in Morse and signalling. The cadets are eager to learn but are handicapped until they are issued with equipment.'

The records do show that the Home Guard used a rifle range in a marl pit situated where Greville Court now is at the top end of St Nicolas Avenue.

Mention of the Home Guard is made in the minutes of the LUDC ARP & National Defence Emergency Committee. The minutes for 14th August 1941 record that the Home Guard dug trenches and erected barbed wire in the King George Field and the church garden. The minutes for 30th October 1941 record that a Home Guard exercise was held on 19th October and highlighted problems with the siting of a number of concrete cylinders agreed between the HG and the Council Engineer and Surveyor. Some endangered the safety of the public and needed re-siting and should be fenced off. The HG replied that it was the Council's responsibility to light these obstructions and suggested luminous paint. The council replied that the persons who placed obstructions on the highway were legally responsible and whilst the Council would be willing to carry out the work the HG should pay for it!

A quote from the Leatherhead Advertiser (December 1940) is:

> Officer to private: 'Why weren't you at roll-call last night?' Private: 'I was making my way back to camp, sir, but it's so well camouflaged, it took me hours to find it.'

One of the major training locations in the country for the HG was the Denbies Estate. Enid Blyton's first husband Hugh Pollock DSO who had joined the HG was appointed Commandant of the War Office School for Instructors of the Home Guard based at Denbies. Pollock won his DSO whilst serving with the Royal Scots Fusiliers in the First World War.

John Gray, aged 11 in 1940, recalls the LDV installing anti-glider posts in his father's fields adjoining the Dorking/Polesden roads and later in the war acting as a runner for the HG during the last school period of the afternoon.

At several locations you can still find the square concrete blocks which were made as wartime anti-tank blocks. This picture shows one at the gates to Bookham Commons

In terms of defences built during the war as a defence against German invasion there are some pillboxes on the southern side of the North Downs but none within Bookham itself. Blocks of concrete were constructed in many places to block roads and these can be seen in the countryside and some of these tank traps remain on Bookham Common.

DETAINEES: KING OF POLAND

Before the war, one character who lived in Little Bookham, Count Geoffrey Potocki of Montalk caused much interest to the locals. The Count was a very controversial man about whom whole books were written. Born in New Zealand he was a Pretender to the Polish Throne and was referred to in the village as the 'King of Poland'. An eccentric who had shoulder length hair, was dressed in long maroon coloured robes and a tricorn hat added a splash of colour to the Bookham scene as he swept through the village or queued at the Post Office. It was alleged that he would return from the Windsor Castle Public House to his home at Half Moon Cottage, balancing a jug of beer on his head. In 1943, acting on information gained from the Polish expatriate community in London, Potocki published the Katyn Manifesto which correctly blamed the massacre on the Soviets. For the British, allied with the Soviets since 1941, the revelations were supremely unwelcome and they continued to maintain that the Nazis had carried out the massacre, although the British government secretly knew the truth. The authorities' response was first to dismiss Potocki as mentally unstable and then to lock him up. Not surprisingly this grave injustice disposed him even less favourably towards the English as works like 'My Private War against England' indicate. History has proven him right on Katyn, but before Potocki is labelled as a wronged visionary it is worth taking another look at that Manifesto. In it he calls upon the Jews 'to repent and behave themselves' (and this was in 1943, when the furnaces of Auschwitz German Concentration Camp were blazing at their brightest). Even before the war Potocki was known for his pro-Nazi views, and was an admirer of the notorious fascist, William Joyce, who broadcast from Germany as 'Lord Haw-Haw' and was later hanged for treason. Potocki was blinded by hatred for the Soviets, and always maintained that as far as Poland was concerned, the Nazis were the lesser of two evils. Even after the war when it became clear that Poland had suffered more than any other nation and the full scale of the holocaust

Count Geoffrey Potocki of Montalk

was known, he maintained that the Nazis were less perpetrators of genocide than victims of defamation. After the war he lived mainly in France where he died in 1996.

HELENA SIKORSKA

As the German armies swept into Poland in 1939 many fled from the country including officials of the government and army. They formed a government in exile initially in Paris and subsequently in London under General Sikorski as their commander in chief. In 1943 while the General was flying in a converted Liberator bomber from Gibraltar the plane somewhat mysteriously lost height and crashed into the harbour. There were rumours that it had been sabotaged which was even the subject of a play in London after the war.

In 1945 General Sikorski's wife Helena moved from London to Maddox Park Farm in Bookham and lived there until shortly before her death in 1972 aged 83. They had one married daughter, Sophia who worked as a secretary to her father and who died with him in the same air crash.

*Helena
Sikorska*

*General
Sikorski
(left) with
Winston
Churchill*

Chapter 4

ENEMY ACTION

Bookham, in common with the whole of the south-east of England, suffered some damage from enemy bombs but owing to its position the amount was relatively small. The war on the Home Front fell into three main periods of activity with 1942-43 being quiet years.

The difficulty in obtaining detailed information on the extent of enemy action is that in order to avoid providing the enemy with useful information the amount publicised at the time was strictly limited. An example occurred in a Leatherhead Advertiser report of October 1940 which stated, 'A landmine dropped by an enemy aeroplane on Sunday evening fell on a well developed village in the Leatherhead area.' Amongst the buildings damaged were the post office and a school. In spite of the damage the post office opened the next day for business. As there is no other reference to a post office in Bookham being damaged, the most likely candidate is Ashtead.

BATTLE OF BRITAIN (July to September 1940)

During this period in the summer of 1940 most of the action was centred around the RAF stations which were to the East and South of Bookham.

There were early skirmishes from 1st July 1940. Initially the Luftwaffe's aim was to disable the British airfields to destroy the RAF fighter capability together with attacks on strategic targets. The activity peaked in Surrey on 27th September. During the battle a significant number of planes were brought down but none in Bookham. After the end of October there was the night Blitz when war in the air changed.

One of the major attacks was that on Brooklands on 4th September. There were planes brought down locally with two at East Horsley and three at Clandon. However the remainder dropped their bombs on the Vickers factory causing 700 casualties and putting production back by two months.

There are no records of any bombs in Bookham during the period from July to late August.

Contrary to popular belief it was the Hurricane, rather than the Spitfire that saved Britain during the dark days of 1940. The majority of German planes shot down during the four month period were destroyed by Hurricanes. The Spitfire was an all metal fighter, slightly faster, had a faster rate of climb and had a higher ceiling, while the Hurricane had a fabric covered fuselage, was quicker to repair and withstood more punishment. However, the Hurricane's unprotected gravity-feed fuel tank in front of the cockpit could rupture when hit, allowing a jet of flame to penetrate the cockpit through the instrument panel, causing serious burn injuries to the pilot. During the war a total of 14,231 Hurricanes and 20,334 Spitfires were produced. The Hurricane was designed at the factory at Brooklands within the motor racing circuit and first flew from Brooklands but was principally manufactured at the Hawker site at Kingston.

The Supermarine
Spitfire

The Hawker
Hurricane

German Aerial Photograph
September 1940

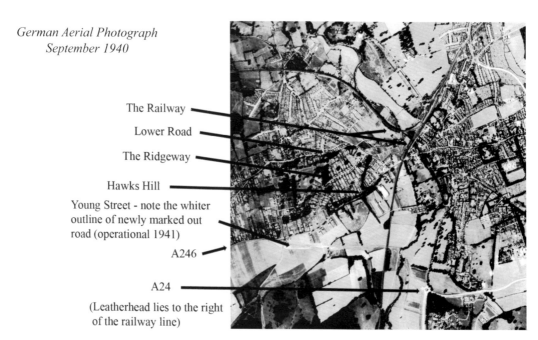

The Railway

Lower Road

The Ridgeway

Hawks Hill

Young Street - note the whiter
outline of newly marked out
road (operational 1941)

A246

A24

(Leatherhead lies to the right
of the railway line)

40

THE BLITZ (August 1940 - May 1941)

This was the period from August 1940 when Hitler ordered the bombing of London and not military targets. Bookham was under the regular flight path and the drone of German aero engines lasted from nightfall until the early hours of the morning. Bookham did not have any significant military targets so, during the Blitz most of the damage was caused by bombers dropping their bombs having failed to reach their specific target.

The first bombs in the district were dropped in Ashtead on 24th and 26th August. On the latter date there were 29 high explosive bombs when 35 houses were damaged and 500 windows smashed. This was the first night of general bombing over London.

Following an air raid on 30th August, the local police reported that 'they had been unable to act as Incident Officers in view of the protection required for personal belongings in wrecked houses'.

Compared with some of the surrounding areas, Bookham received little bomb damage. One of the two worst incidents, which is still vividly remembered by Turville Kille's son, who was then eight years old, was on Friday 13th September 1940, when a stick of 19 bombs was dropped from Downs Way towards the High Street. The barber's shop in Beckley Parade was partially demolished while the barber was cutting the hair of the brother-in law of Turville Kille (Snr). As Turville later commented "you might say they had a close shave because they escaped injury." A pre-fabricated hut was built on the site providing accommodation for the Bookham Auxiliary Fire Service.

The second worst incident occurred on 19th October 1940 when 12 bombs were dropped in a line from Southey Hall to the Leatherhead by-pass, damaging shops, offices and houses. Two bombs fell on oil storage tanks at the Waterworks in Leatherhead and burning oil seeped through the drains

A German Heinkel 111 dropping its bombs in 1940

into the River Mole, the fire taking almost a day to put out. When the land was subsequently developed for apartments there were problems as the residual oil had not been fully dealt with. Badingham College was also damaged along with the bridge over the railway at Fetcham. Some houses in The Glade, Fetcham, were destroyed and two bungalows in The Street suffered the same fate. There were four casualties, but elsewhere this Saturday was described as one of the quietest days during the Blitz.

The small round ponds at various locations on the common are the result of bombs dropped by enemy aircraft. In other places bomb craters can be seen such as at the top of Woodlands Road.

One evacuee, 6½ years old when war started, came to Great Bookham in 1939 from New Eltham in Kent and lived in a house in Dowlans Road with its back garden bordering Farmer Gray's 40 acre field. Days were spent in blissful ignorance of the dangers of war and he and his friends watched dogfights in the skies during the Battle of Britain. They rooted around the odd bomb crater and collected shrapnel which became something of a currency to be exchanged or haggled over depending upon its perceived worth. Another of his friends managed to get hold of a complete

"Coo! Who wants conkers – we're collectin' shrapnel!"

(Punch Goes to War 1939-1945)

incendiary bomb which he brought to school in his satchel and which was greatly admired. A teacher spotted this war memento and called in an air raid warden to dispose of it. It was only later that he learned what burning magnesium could do and the realisation sank in of the blood curdling dangers to which they had exposed themselves and their families.

On 24th September a Heinkel 111, straying from a mission in the East End

Now a pond but originally a bomb crater

(Beckton Gasworks) dumped its bombs, one destroying a house in Bookham. It was then caught in the searchlights of 460 Battery of the Royal Artillery based at Weybridge. For the local anti-aircraft gunners the Heinkel was a sitting duck and they scored several direct hits including one that took away the entire tail. The engines landed in the grounds of the Gordon Boys' Home at Chobham and the fuselage came down on the recreation ground where it burned out. The crash occurred at 01.37 hrs. The press were invited to photograph the following day and the picture shows soldiers examining the wreckage. The crew of four were all captured and interrogated.

A Mr Dicker was the head gardener/gatekeeper at Southey Hall School and he had one or two local men from the village to help him. The kitchen garden provided nearly all the vegetables for the school. He and Mrs Dicker lived in the lodge by the main gate (where the bungalow at no 182A Lower Road now stands) until a German bomb destroyed it on 24th October 1940. Thankfully they were both taken out of the wreckage unhurt. Mr Dicker did not seem worried about the house but was cross that he could not find his false teeth! About a week later a land mine fell in the grounds and these were the incidents

The original gates to Southey Hall still stand at 182A Lower Road

Inspecting the German Heinkel 111 that was shot down and crashed at Chobham

to cause Southey Hall School to evacuate to Dunsford near Exeter.

There was an RAF plane that came down on 29th October in Leatherhead when it ran out of fuel. The pilot's CO criticised him for not making more effort to glide to a runway.

On 7th January 1941 a 3000lb unexploded bomb was blown up near Bookham Station.

Later in 1941 a bomb damaged St Nicolas Church including the churchyard wall, the clock and the East window. In March 1942 it was decided that no action would be taken until the War Damage Commission had communicated with them although there was a local appeal towards costs. Historic glass was purchased in 1954 from Costessey Hall in Norfolk and the window was finally replaced in 1958.

After a bomb fell in Dowlans Road it was reported that the whole area looked as if it was covered in snow - this being caused by the displacement of chalk.

Replacement East Window at St Nicolas Church

John Gray (farmer Gray's son) recalls a low-flying German aircraft machine-gunning Goldstone Farm, where he then lived, just before Christmas 1941. The bullets passed through two doors of an outbuilding into a large heap of artificial fertiliser which had to be sieved before use. The aircraft flew off towards Epsom.

For a day by day account of enemy action over Bookham see Appendix B.

V1 FLYING BOMB AND V2 ROCKET (June 1944 toApril 1945)

This period lasted from June 1944 to April 1945 when severe damage was caused by these flying bombs and rockets. There were two types of unmanned bombs launched in the second half of 1944 and early 1945, the V1 and the V2.

*V1 on
its
launch
pad*

*A V1 in
flight*

V1 - THE DOODLEBUG

The first type was the V1 (Vergeltungswaffen, 'weapon of reprisal') an unmanned flying bomb and which was mainly targeted over Kent towards London. They were known as 'buzz bombs' or 'doodlebugs'. The V1 carried one ton of high explosive and travelled at a maximum speed of 400 mph and had a maximum flying distance of 200 miles but the weather could decrease this. A pre-set magnetic compass and gyroscopic auto-pilot determined and maintained its course. A small propeller at the front of the weapon registered the distance covered and at a pre-set distance, the guidance system caused the V1 to go into a steep dive. The abrupt change in attitude interrupted the fuel supply to the engine and the V1 exploded on impact wherever it fell.

Dorothy Joce, who was one of the principals of the Spinney School writes in her memoirs, 'Life Begins at 90'.

" .... the 'alerts' lasted for much longer and sometimes went on all day.... the general memory of the last few weeks of term is the continual hearing of them.....I shall never forget the last Friday morning of that summer term when five times during that morning we called 'rabbits in your holes' and the children dived under their desks. Fortunately we all treated it as great fun."

The coming of the doodlebugs clearly had a significant impact on the local community. Many of those living in Bookham at that time remember vividly the sound of the V1s or seeing them. One

A German poster produced aiming to terrorise Britain into submission

person remembers that they were painted green. Another, a pupil at Manor House School, saw one through a glass roof as it was passing overhead (this could well have been the V1 which destroyed a house in Effingham Common Road and which killed a relation of one of the youngsters at the Spinney School). Dorothy records this as having happened on 10th July 1944. She also recalls:

".....the most nerve-racking time for me was in driving home after school the children who lived on Effingham Common. With my back to the direction from which the flying bombs came I could neither hear nor see if anything was happening and was thankful to get them all safely delivered and turn and drive home facing a clear sky."

Throughout England 9,251 V1s were plotted between 13th June 1944 and 29th March 1945. Early on there was little defence. The highest number on a single day was 161 on 2nd July 1944. In late July 1944 artillery was moved to the South Coast and this left a space for aircraft to attack them without the risk of friendly fire. The last defence comprised two thousand barrage balloons. The V1s were sufficiently slow that later in the war, in March 1945, artillery hit 86 out of 125. The devastation in London and Kent was immense. As an example, by the time the main onslaught ceased on 24th August 1944, not a single house or building in Penge in south east London, an area of some seven hundred acres, was left undamaged.

At 11.33am on 6th July a V1 fell opposite Effingham Golf club. Some properties in Woodlands Road were affected by the blast.

Only three V1s are listed as having landed in Bookham in 1944. Two V1s landed near the railway, one at Maddox Park on 3rd August which damaged one house seriously and seventy slightly but with no casualties and another on 12th October near Bayfield (now the Bookham Grange Hotel) where twenty five houses were slightly damaged. The third was to the north of Bookham Common towards Slyfield.

The effect of the V1s was limited as they could be shot out of the sky by anti-aircraft fire as the guns could lock onto the trajectory of the incoming V1 with early warning gunlaying radar and predictor systems. Fighter planes were also used to flip the V1 over so that it headed straight for the ground. Over 50% of the V1s fired at Britain were destroyed before they crashed to the ground and exploded.

V2 ROCKET

The second type of unmanned bomb was the V2, a rocket with a maximum speed of 3,500 mph. The first fell on 28th September 1944 and the total number reported was 1,115. Because of their speed there did not appear to be any effective counter measures except destroying their manufacture

V2 on its mobile launcher

*A V2 Rocket
just fired*

or for the allies capturing the launch sites which was not done until March 1945. Only one fell in the local area, in Park Lane, Ashtead, causing one casualty and damaging fifty houses.

After the war many of the German V2 designers emigrated to America and formed the foundation team to design and manufacture the space rockets of today.

It is worth stating that the invention of bombs was not all one sided and that one of our more notable inventors lived in the adjoining parish of Effingham. Sir Barnes Neville Wallis, CBE, FRS, RDI, FRAeS (26th September 1887 – 30th October 1979), was an English scientist, engineer and inventor and is best known for inventing the bouncing bomb used by the RAF in Operation Chastise to attack the dams of the Ruhr Valley during WWII. Among his other inventions were the geodetic airframe of the Wellington bomber and the earthquake bomb. He lived with his family at White Hill House (now Little Court),

Sir Neville Barnes Wallis

49

Beech Avenue, Effingham for 49 years from 1930 until his death in 1979. He is buried at St Lawrence's Church, Effingham.

BOOKHAM RESIDENT CASUALTIES

The total Bookham resident casualty list from WW II amounted to twenty one, eighteen of whom were killed on active service. Of the remaining three, one was in the Home Guard, one was a policeman, and the other, particularly sadly, was a 14 year old boy. There are twelve specific WWII memorials in St Nicolas churchyard and none at Little Bookham Church. Six of the casualties are commemorated only at or near their place of death. This is in stark contrast to the number of Bookham resident casualties arising from the First World War amounting to thirty-nine, all of whom are assumed to have been killed on active service. Thirty-four are named on the war memorial at St Nicolas Church, and a further five at Little Bookham Church. This amounts to a significant proportion of the population of the Bookhams at that time. Further details of Bookham resident casualties are provided in Appendix D.

WHERE BOMBS FELL

The map on the next page shows where bombs fell in central Bookham. Three types of bomb are marked:

Explosive: 250kg or 500kg high explosive bombs

Incendiary: Small bombs filled with a highly inflammable chemical such as phosphorus or napalm

Oil: Incendiary device but filled with petroleum oil

A full bomb map of the Leatherhead district can be seen at the Leatherhead Museum.

●	Explosive
▲	Incendiary
■	Oil

Chapter 5

BOOKHAM LIFE DURING THE WAR

Once the war commenced it is clear that shopkeepers were under considerable pressure dealing with rationing, shortages in food supplies often as a result of enemy action affecting their suppliers, and the impact of supplying evacuees.

RATIONING - FOOD

It was one of the principal strategies of the Axis to attack shipping bound for the United Kingdom, restricting British industry and potentially starving the nation into submission. To deal with sometimes extreme shortages the Ministry of Food instituted a system of rationing. Each family had to register at a particular shop, for example with a grocer and a butcher. Buff coloured books were issued to adults and green for small children and babies. The latter books were prized possessions as they entitled the owner to extra milk. The ration limits were varied from time to time. Coupons were issued for biscuits and one resident recalled them being counted out from a huge tin at the grocers. Hansons, the bakers used to make Swiss rolls for sale on Saturdays and it was a matter of 'first come, first served'. On a romantic note, it is believed that one married couple met for the first time in the queue!

The ration per adult per week was at it lowest in 1940/41 due to the results of enemy action. Thereafter, the limits varied according to supplies. Fish remained unrationed. For obvious reasons, such fruits as bananas and oranges were very

Wartime Food Ration Book

rarely available. The following was the allocation of rationed food per person per week (unless stated differently):

Bacon and ham	4oz (100g)
Meat	to the value of 1s.2d (6p today).
	Sausages were not rationed but difficult to get; offal (liver, kidneys, tripes) was originally unrationed but sometimes formed part of the meat ration.
Cheese	2oz (50g) sometimes it went up to 4oz (100g) and even up to 8oz (225g).
Margarine	4oz (100g)
Butter	2oz (50g)
Milk	3 pints (1800ml) occasionally dropping to 2 pints (1200ml). Household milk (skimmed or dried) was available : 1 packet per four weeks.
Sugar	8oz (225g). There were one or two ways this could be made to go further. For instance there was a recipe for Beetroot Pudding:
	'Just the job to make your sugar ration go further! First mix flour and baking powder, rub in the margarine, then add sugar and grated beetroot. Now mix all the ingredients to a soft cake consistency with 3 or 4 tablespoons of milk. Add a few drops of flavouring essence if you have it. Turn the mixture into a greased pie dish or tin and bake in a moderate oven for 35 minutes. This pudding tastes equally good hot or cold.'
Jam	1lb (450g) every two months.
Tea	2oz (50g).
Eggs	1 fresh egg a week if available but often only one every two weeks. Dried eggs 1 packet every four weeks.
Sweets	12oz (350g) every four weeks

In Bookham as in the rest of the country housewives received food parcels from the Dominions and USA. Others worked to become self sufficient - thanks to their skills in the garden and on the allotment. Recipes for such items as carrot jam and nettle tea also became popular. The unattractiveness of dried eggs encouraged people to keep chickens themselves. However, this did lead to some chicken rustling. The solution of keeping geese as a deterrent was only partially successful as in one local incident the geese were stolen along with the chickens.

At a time when ingredients for both the making and icing of cakes were totally unavailable, cardboard wedding cakes were available for hire with the 'icing' being made of chalk!

FOOD SUPPLIES

Food Rationing required ingenuity on the part of housewives to provide nutritious meals. Other than the items of food which were rationed, as food in general became less easy to acquire, it is clear that many residents were growing much of their own food and that bartering took place, e.g. cooking apples, rhubarb, eggs and many vegetables. Prior to the war there had been a surprising reliance on imported food (as much as 70%) and then as a result of enemy action most had to be home grown. All fruit of overseas origin became unobtainable.

To encourage the public to keep chickens, it was decided that up to 25 birds could be kept before there was a stipulation that eggs had to be sold to the Ministry of Food. The Bookham Poultry Club advertised 'Plucking and Trussing Demonstrations'.

Advert from a Bookhams Bulletin of the time

A Rabbit Club was also established in Bookham and district. The Ministry of Agriculture sponsored 'domestic rabbit clubs' and made an allowance of food to all breeders provided they were members of organised clubs. Breeders with more than four breeding does were regarded as commercial producers and allowed a ration of 28lbs of bran per quarter for every four does – subject to certain conditions. Pets were excluded from the scheme!

In September 1942 it was decided to set up a Bookham Goat Club to 'foster goat-keeping and to encourage the improvement of stock, having special regard for wartime conditions'. Two months after the club was established, it had a membership of forty-two. Members only paid 10/- for stud fees. It was then possible to obtain a ration for six months for kids when the owner had more than one milch goat and up to twelve

DIG FOR VICTORY

months if there was only one other goat kept. Representations were made to the Surrey War Agriculture Committee regarding the slowness in the issue of feeding stuff coupons. It was proposed to hold a Goat Club Show in conjunction with the show staged by Great and Little Bookham Garden Society.

Milk continued to be delivered. There was a report of a court case in which William Perry, a milk roundsman was summoned for allowing his horse to bolt down Groveside. Only four shillings costs were awarded against him as he said that his horse had been stung on the nose by a wasp!

Food production was of course vital due to the heavy losses sustained by ships carrying food as a result of German submarine activity – hence the slogan 'Dig for Victory'. On local farms extra land was ploughed for food production and Land Army girls provided valuable help.

Bookham Sewage Works had a crop of potatoes in October 1941 but found difficulty in having it harvested (a hundred and twenty tons). It was suggested that teams of senior boys and wardens be recruited but there is no record of the result of the appeal. It was agreed that the land be rented out for growing wheat to 'professional farmers' who had the necessary equipment.

The LUDC resolved to thank the officer commanding the Cameron Highlanders of Ottawa for their willing help in potato planting at the allotment at the Little Bookham sewage works. It was agreed to purchase 4.5 tons of artificial fertiliser for use there.

Permission was given for workers in the Old Barn Hall to cultivate a portion of the land adjoining the hall.

A soup kitchen was opened at the rear of the Victoria Hotel.

'Pig Bins' were provided for the collection of vegetable peelings and other food waste in most roads in the two villages as well as outside the Old Barn Hall.

OTHER RATIONING

Clothing

Clothing was also severely rationed and sometimes residents would undo old jumpers to provide wool to knit into new garments. 'Segs' or 'Blakeys' – metal strips – were nailed onto the soles of shoes to save the leather from wearing out. Apparently army blankets occasionally came up for sale at £1 each and these were dyed and used to make coats.

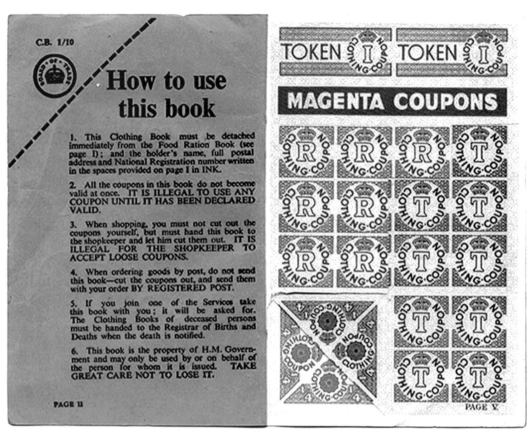

Clothing Coupon Book

It was specified when clothes rationing was introduced in June 1941 that every man, woman and child should be given sixty-six coupons to last for a year (later reduced to sixty). Coupons varied according to the size of the garment, for example a woman typically would require fourteen coupons for an overcoat while a man required thirteen for a jacket and eight for a pair of trousers. An average family would spend about £30 per annum on clothes however a utility suit by itself for a man would cost £30. Everyone was encouraged to 'Make do and mend'.

The Utility Clothing Scheme was set up by the Government in response to the shortage of clothing materials and labour due to the requirements of the war effort. Apparently, the Board of Trade sponsored the creation of ranges of 'Utility Clothing' which had to meet tight specifications as to the amount of material and labour used. For example, it was specified in 1942 that skirts were to be shorter and there should be no double breasted coats and jackets as well as no sleeve buttons or turn-ups on trousers. These clothes were labelled with a government 'utility mark' (U41 also known as the 'two cheeses'). Later in a similar way the 'Utility Furniture Scheme' was established in order to ensure that the most efficient use was made of scarce timber.

Soap

All types of soap were rationed. Coupons were allotted by weight or (if liquid) by quantity. In 1945 the ration gave four coupons each month; babies, some workers and invalids were allowed more. One coupon would yield either:

4 oz bar hard soap

3 oz bar toilet soap

½oz liquid soap

6 oz soft soap

3 oz soap flakes

6 oz soap powder

Fuel

The Fuel and Lighting (Coal) Order 1941 came into force in January 1942. Central heating was prohibited in the summer months.

Domestic coal was rationed to 50 cwt (hundredweight) a year or approximately 1cwt per week..

Coal did not come off ration until 1958, four years after the rationing of other goods.

Paper

Newspapers were limited from September 1939 at first to 60% of their pre-war consumption of newsprint and by 1945 to 25% of their pre-war consumption. Wrapping paper for most goods was prohibited.

Howard Weale in Little Bookham Street was also the local coal merchant

The paper shortage often made it more difficult than usual for authors to get books published.

HOT WATER BOTTLES

A general instruction was given in 1944 stating that private individuals requiring a rubber hot water bottle must obtain a 'medical certificate stating their age and nature of the disease'. This had to be submitted to the Ministry of Health who, if appropriate would authorise a local retailer to supply the applicant from stock. Stone hot water bottles enjoyed a renaissance and were in great demand!

RADIO

The radio was a constant companion. The BBC was responsible not only for keeping people informed about the progress of the war but also for keeping their spirits up. The Home Service provided hours of dance music, variety and comedy shows. 'Workers' Playtime' and 'Music While You Work' were regular favourites with Vera Lynn the 'Forces Sweetheart' the most popular singer of the war. Comedy programmes like ITMA ('It's that Man Again' - a reference taken from a Daily Express headline referring to Hitler) with Tommy Handley and Kenneth Horne's 'Much Binding in the Marsh' were listened to avidly.

Other broadcasts were also tuned into in war time Britain, including those by William Joyce 'Lord Haw-Haw' which were transmitted from Berlin..."Jairmany calling. Jairmany calling". William Joyce is believed to have lived in Bookham in Marden Hill at one time. There is a report of one of his broadcasts in which he suggested that if the housewives of Bookham went down to Madges the Butchers in Church Road they would find he was out of liver!

Tommy Handley - 'It's that man again'

Vera Lynn - the Forces Sweetheart - "We'll meet again..."

William Joyce - Lord 'Haw-Haw'

NATIONAL REGISTRATION - THE 1939 IDENTITY CARD

As war approached, preparations were made to enable a national register to be rapidly compiled and identity cards issued. A National Registration Bill was quickly introduced and royal assent given on the 5th September 1939, just two days after the declaration of war and a few days later it was announced that National Registration Day would be Friday 29th September 1939.

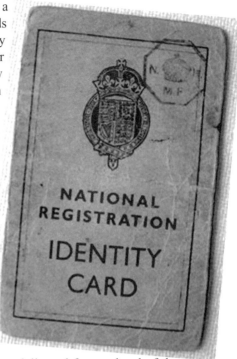

Three main reasons were put forward by the government for passing the law. The first was the major dislocation caused by mobilisation and mass evacuation and the wartime need for complete manpower control and planning in order to maximise the efficiency of the war economy. The second was the likelihood of rationing, actually introduced from January 1940 onwards and the third main reason was that the Government needed recent statistics about the population. As the last census had been held in 1931 there was little accurate data on which to base vital planning decisions.

The decision was made to use similar methods as for the census for which planning had started for the 1941 census. Basically 65,000 enumerators across the country delivered forms ahead of the chosen day. On the 29th householders were required to record details on the registration forms and then on the following Sunday and Monday enumerators visited every householder, checked the form and there and then issued a completed identity card for each resident.

Information gathered for each person was their address, name, sex, date of birth, marital condition, occupation and whether a member of the armed forces or reserves.

Approximately 46 million cards were issued. The identity card had two pages and at the top of each page the enumerator entered the person's name and their identity card number. This card number consisted of a four letter enumeration district code plus the line number of the schedule that was completed by the enumerator so for area ABCD, schedule line 24, 3rd person in the household the card number would have been 'ABCD 24/3'. In fact to this day some 70 plus years later those issued with such a number can be used as an alternative to the National Insurance Number of today.

CHURCHES IN WARTIME

In the St Nicolas Parish Magazine of October 1939 the Rector stated, "The struggle is to allow men to worship freely, to live peaceably, to learn to appreciate the true goods of life: kindness, sympathy, mutual co-operation, knowledge, beauty. We are struggling against a power that seeks to shape by force men's thoughts and to shape them in evil mould. We can only succeed by training ourselves in that truth that makes us free." He also made the remark that everyone was 'living under conditions of complete tension'. In the following year he commented on the people's state of mind which had resulted 'in tiredness owing to the conditions under which we live' and suggested that 'you should brace yourselves for the present and train yourselves for the future'.

From the Parochial Church Council minutes for both Great and Little Bookham Churches together with records of the Baptist and Congregational Churches it is difficult to believe that a world war was in fact taking place. The Parochial Church Council at St Nicolas spent lengthy sessions arguing over the inadequacies of the organ which had been installed just prior to the war, and who was going to pay for the repairs, as well as discussions concerning disputes with the tenant of part of the churchyard. Barely a reference appears to the fact that a world war was raging. However, it was noted that on occasions, 'air activity did thin the congregations.'

Soon after the commencement of war Church House (the hall for St Nicolas Church) in Lower Road which has long since been demolished and replaced by flats was sequestrated for 'war purposes' and allocated for use initially by the ARP. Church House was also advertised for use as a First Aid Post and for dances and whist drives. A claim was submitted by the church for compensation and judging by the amount of discussion it was clearly regarded as a 'big issue' at the time. The Congregational Church which in 1972 became the United Reformed Church also received a request from the Surrey Education Committee for the use of their hall for out-of-hours activities for 'London children evacuated to Bookham' at a rental of £1 per week plus 10s for cleaning and also a request from the County Health Officer for it to be used for a fortnightly clinic. It was also agreed that the Canadian Forces could utilise the premises as a 'Rest Centre', particularly as a 'Reading and Writing Room' but this appears to have been little used.

Church House as a hall as it was until just after the war. It faced Lower Road and on the right can be seen the garage which is now White's Garage. Notice the open fields of Sole Farm behind the hall on which (in 1958) the bungalows and houses of The Garstons were built

St Nicolas Church

*All Saints Church
Little Bookham*

*Congregational Church
Now the United Reform
Church*

*Memorial Village Hall in
Lower Road 1912. It became
the Baptist Church in 1929.*

Strict fire regulations were laid down by the Guildford Diocese concerning the care of churches in wartime which stipulated that all ancient plate, registers and the like should be in a place of safety, for example a bank. They were instructed to keep the church under observation in case of fire. Particularly interesting and surprising was the instruction which reads 'Copies on microfilm to be made of all Parish Registers and copies to be deposited in a place of safety for the duration of the war'.

Under a Government Scheme of War Damage Insurance, no premiums were payable by churches in respect of the fabric as all damage was to be made good from Government funds after the end of the war. However, premiums had to be paid to cover all the many fixtures and fittings including organs, screens and pews.

Church Services and Ceremonies

The registers for the various churches indicate that their services continued much as normal and that numbers in the congregations were maintained. At St Nicolas for example in 1940 the total number receiving communion was 6,700 but in the month of May 1941 alone there were 974 communicants. On one occasion in that month there was a crowded Morning Service at which they 'were particularly pleased to welcome the Home Guard and a detachment from the RASC (Royal Army Service Corps)'. There was also quite a close bond with the Canadian Army units based locally and at Easter 1941 the full congregation included a detachment of Canadian soldiers. The Parish Magazine stated: 'We wonder how many of our Canadian friends realised that they were receiving from a chalice that has been in use amongst the people of Great Bookham since the year in which the Hudson's Bay Company was first formed'. In 1942, a special preacher at St Nicolas was Canon Hepburn, Deputy Assistant Principal Chaplain to the Canadian Army Overseas.

St Nicolas held 114 weddings with at least eleven in which the bridegroom was a member of the Canadian forces and 257 baptisms of which at least 13 were recorded as having a father from Canada. One significant funeral recorded in the Register was that of Mary Ann Stacey of 8 Beckley Cottages, Leatherhead Road who had died in November 1942 aged 101 years and four weeks (born 5th October 1841).

Christmas was celebrated in the Bookhams as well as possible during the war years although limitations on food supplies must have had a considerable effect. At Christmas 1940 it was stated that 'at St Nicolas, in spite of lighting restrictions we managed very well and are glad to report an increase in communicants (364). As usual, the church looked very beautiful in its Christmas dress and the effect of each celebration with the chancel dimly lighted and the rest of the church in darkness was most impressive'.

The St Nicolas Church Sunday School also continued throughout the war. In April 1941 the Rector commented that 'there had been an improvement in the numbers attending, recovering from its difficulties due to the air raids.' At that stage he was pleased to report that there had been an increase in the number of teachers from amongst the senior girls. In the same year an experiment was being tried to take infants too young for Sunday School into the Choir Vestry 'where they are provided with some small chairs and can practise singing without detriment to the rest of the congregation'!

Each year St Nicolas Church arranged a Sunday School treat in the Baptist Hall at which up to 160 attended including a party from the School of Stitchery and Lace in Rectory Lane. The programme usually included community singing, films, demonstrations of scout activities, a shadowgraph and a conjuror plus, of course, the tea. Various comments were made as to how the organiser, Mrs Madge the wife of the butcher, 'got round Lord Woolton' the Minister of Food. In a time of considerable restriction and rationing, in 1942 for example, 200 doughnuts appeared. The remark was made: 'We did not think that such things existed.'

The church choirs continued throughout the war and in July 1940 the Congregational Church held its annual concert. It was well supported and a collection raised the sum of £2 12s, £2 3s of which was donated to the British Sailors' Society.

Some reports produced by the various churches summarise the ways in which the churches, and also the Bookham community in general, were affected when 'a new chapter began one Sunday in September 1939 - the call up of some of the younger men and women to the services and other wartime duties and having to contend with blackouts, rationing, some bombing and, in general, bad news'. Despite this the churches were very active and reports recall many 'unforgettable services', some involving the Canadian servicemen. At St Nicolas it was commented that 'there were many hindrances to attending services due to 'the increasing number of Sunday activities imposed on old and young alike'.

In September 1940, the Rector stated in the St Nicolas Parish Magazine – 'Bookham has had its first real attack from the air. We should indeed be ungrateful people if we did not return thanks for the complete absence of injury to individuals and the relatively small amount of injury to property'. In December 1940 there was further comment in the same publication – 'We continue to be very much in the thick of it as far as airplane attack is concerned and some evenings have been rather more exciting than most of us care about. We have much to be thankful for in being spared casualties to date but we deeply sympathise with those whose homes have been wrecked or damaged'.

In November 1940, the Rector remarked that 'the Clergy, in common with all who have charge of children, have been placed in a very difficult position by the attitude of authority over the meaning of the siren. Originally, we were told that on the giving of the alarm, children should be moved to trenches. The instructions were clear and we rehearsed our Sunday School in what to do. It now seems to have been realised that during the day the siren goes many times without the slightest sign of a raider as far as a district like this is concerned and to spend all the time in the trenches will be harmful both mentally and physically to the children. Those in authority have accordingly been told that they must use discretion over moving the children. They are given no guidance as to how that discretion is to be used'. It was noted that 'the latest schools to be given protection, instead of trenches, a room is sheltered against blast by walls outside the openings. On this analogy, our church is the best shelter possible with its extremely thick outer walls and the heavy pews to get under'!

In August 1941, the extension to the St Nicolas Churchyard was consecrated by Bishop Golding-Bird. It is understood that supplies of the Order of Service had been printed but all had been burnt during an air raid in London on the previous day. Coincidentally the collection taken on the day was to go to 'The Lord Mayor's Fund for Air Raid Distress'.

Overall Impact of Rationing

The scarcity of food and the restrictions caused by rationing were biting deeply into the average family's way of life. One remark was also made that 'the trivial restrictions and deprivations imposed on us by the War have already so become part of our daily life that they are no longer irksome. It is as natural to carry an identity card as it is to have a clean handkerchief, a gas mask is an indisputable part of our travelling wardrobe and the nightly locking and dismembering of our cars have become practically automated'.

THE OLD BARN HALL

The Old Barn Hall played a crucial role in the life of the villages in the war years and was a focal point for many activities as it remains today.

Food Provision

During September 1939 a canteen was established at the Old Barn Hall run by the WVS under the auspices of the Leatherhead UDC to feed some of the 600 evacuees billeted in the neighbourhood. These included the pupils of the Strand School evacuated from Tulse Hill to premises sited in Browns Lane, Effingham. The Strand pupils walked across the fields daily to the hall, as well as weekly to the recreation ground for games lessons. In the first instance, between 170 and 180 dinners were provided each day in two sittings. Later when at its peak, the canteen was capable of providing 1,500 meals per week. For a charge of four pence a meal the children received two courses of English staple foods such as roast beef, potatoes and vegetables with typically college pudding, steam pudding or tapioca pudding as dessert. Each child received a ration of a pennyworth of meat. The prunes and custard served on Fridays was said to be 'legendary', although the semolina is remembered as 'tasting like soap'. The work was overseen by Mrs Bowen of the WVS who was highly regarded by all, with a team of up to 60 helpers working in three shifts. Apart from a paid cook, workers were entirely voluntary and as a result the canteen 'paid its way'. They kept going despite all the difficulties, even when the main services were cut off as a result of bomb damage. The children from the village also had their meals at the hall as well but at a different sitting. There would appear to have been some rivalry between them and the Strand pupils.

A comment was made in 1942 that 'Go down Church Street on any Monday to Friday about 11.30am and just about the entrance to The Park, you suddenly become hungry, a most savoury smell has crept up your nostrils. Turn left and follow your nose and you reach its origin – the Old Barn Hall Canteen'.

Shortly after opening the canteen teas were served for visiting parents and friends at a small charge and then meals for adults for eight pence.

In March 1940 the Canteen Sub-Committee considered a report on a major disaster: the accidental breakage of 54 cups, 5 saucers, 42 large plates, 43 soup plates and 1 large bowl to the value of £3. The staff had offered to organise a whist drive to raise the money but the Sub-Committee contrived to find the cash from its contingency funds.

When it was practical food for the canteen was purchased centrally. In May 1940 for example the

The Old Barn Hall

prices for staple items were: bread: 8d per quartern-loaf (a four pound loaf); milk: 2/- per gallon up to 6 gallons and 1/10 thereafter; and potatoes 9/- per hundredweight.

The official policy was the provision of Communal Feeding Centres in order that meals could be prepared more efficiently and the Community Kitchens Committee examined sites within population centres such as Ashtead, Leatherhead and Bookham with a view to establishing a British Restaurant. It was agreed that the Bookham School Canteen could merge with a British Restaurant to obtain the benefits of BR's central supplies both for food and equipment. An application was made to the Ministry of Food who rejected the application as there appeared to be no over-riding demand at that stage. On LUDC's insistence, they did agree that food could be purchased by the public on a cash-and-carry basis and consumed in an old wooden building to be erected as an annex to the main building of the Old Barn Hall.

Other Uses of the Old Barn Hall

The Old Barn Hall was used for a variety of purposes, even boxing evenings were staged.

The Citizens Advice Bureau was open in the hall three days each week for two hours in the early part of the war, very valuable in being able to advise on the growing amount of legislation, for example concerning rationing, war damage claims, grants and even the supply of utility furniture.

Bookham Youth Club was permitted to use the Old Barn Hall free of charge to stage shows in aid of the Lord Lieutenant's Fund. It was decided in November 1939 that the caretaker would not be given extra wages despite the extra work falling to him because of the presence of the evacuees.

The hall was regularly used for social events including dances by the Canadian forces, stationed in the area. It is understood from one participant that the girls attending were collected from the surrounding areas in a lorry, taken to the hall, and sometimes to dances at Southey Hall, and returned afterwards. The popular band, for this and at other local venues, was led by Henry Griffiths, organist at St Nicolas Church who apparently was blind. The Canadians were described as 'well mannered' and, 'being very sociable, this livened up the dances no end'. On New Year's Eve 1944 the hall which, as a converted barn did not have the later extensions and permanent stage that is seen today, was packed with 185 people including many Canadians. It was stated that 'you could hardly see across the room for smoke and the dancers were packed solid'.

One girl recalled going straight to the hall for a dance still dressed in her gym slip. In 1943 Bookham and Effingham Youth Committee stated that they wanted to prevent 13 to 15 year old girls from attending the dances staged for the troops. When approached, Surrey County Council replied that 'no action could be taken as there were no powers to attach to the dance licence'.

In November 1942, the Old Barn Hall received a demand from the Performing Rights Society for the sum of six guineas.

The Old Barn Hall accommodated a Surrey Council Clinic which used an adjacent cowman's cottage as well.

The British Restaurant transferred to the Old Barn Hall from the Victoria Hotel in 1943, when the ARP and the Home Guard also left, at a stage when it was considered that the threat of invasion had reduced.

THE BRITISH RESTAURANT

These communal kitchens were created by the Ministry of Food early in the war 'to ensure that communities and people who had run out of coupons were still able to eat'. Miss Patricia M.Cooper was appointed by the Leatherhead Urban District Council (LUDC) in April 1941, as Communal Feeding Organiser in consequence of the council's decision to embark upon a programme of establishing British Restaurants (BR) to serve the four wards within the Urban District (Ashtead, Bookham, Fetcham and Leatherhead).

Miss Cooper was required in the first place to prepare schemes for the establishment of four British Restaurants, including planning and layout, in consultation with the Engineer and Surveyor, provision of equipment, staffing and organisation and supervision of the meals service.

The first British Restaurant was opened in the centre of Leatherhead on 5th June 1941, the second at Ashtead in October 1941, the third in Fetcham in May 1942, and the fourth in Bookham in September 1942. From their inception to the date of Miss Cooper's resignation, the restaurants served 385,000 meals. Her duties at the time of her resignation comprised the supervision

Patricia Cooper
Communal Feeding Organiser

66

and management of the following:

Four British Restaurants

Four school canteens (with meals distributed to two additional feeding centres)

County Rescue School Canteen

Rural Residents' Meat Pie Scheme

Civil Defence Meals Service

The Bookham British Restaurant, mainly a cash and carry meals service was opened at the Victoria Hotel at the top of the High Street. Initially some 36 to 39 meals were served each day and it was stated that 'it is hoped that more people will support this service which the Bookham people have asked to be provided'. By the end of that year, the average had increased to 73 per day and by June 1943, 116 per day. It was noted that the scheme 'is intended to stimulate the national economy, both in food and fuel, and is at the disposal of all'. Customers were asked to bring their own bowls and plates on which the food could be served and taken away to be eaten at home. 'Food for all the members of the family' could be had at the 'moderate' price of 9d per meal, later increased to 10d. The service also worked the 'Rural Pie Scheme' at 4d each, originally introduced mainly for agricultural workers who could not get home to a mid-day meal. 1,000 pies were being served per week and in September 1943 the manufacture of the pies was transferred to Little Bookham Village Hall to relieve the pressure.

It was suggested also that the BR should be closed on a Saturday and that customers bought an extra pie on Friday for consumption on the following day. In 1943 a scheme for upgrading the British Restaurant and Pie Centre was considered by the Council but the estimated cost of £2,954 was regarded as being too high and a refurbishment plan for £30 was approved. However, in April 1944 the use of a Nissen Hut, instead of Nashcrete recommended by the Ministry of Food, was recommended at a cost of £2,500 but the Ministry deferred a decision for three months pending a review of the whole BR service.

Whilst the restaurant was open there had been a problem with rats and the use of a rat destruction contractor employed through the County Council

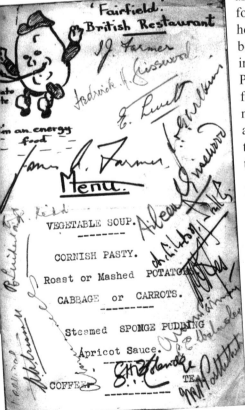

Autographed menu at farewell pary for Miss P Cooper

was approved and the cost of £12 per annum was considered appropriate.

By early 1945 the restaurant was still making a loss and the closing down of the whole operation was proposed. Comment was made that if this were to happen local shops could still sell pies made by BR.

BLOOD DONORS

In March 1941 an appeal was made by the staff of Bookham First Aid Post for blood donors as blood was urgently needed in considerable quantities for use in hospitals, military, civil or maternity.

LITTLE BOOKHAM VILLAGE HALL

Little Bookham Village Hall

The Little Bookham Village Hall (built after 1912 on land donated by the well known local resident, Mrs Chrystie) was also used for a wide range of social and community activities during the war years as well as for the manufacture of pies when this operation was transferred from the Old Barn Hall during 1943.

WOMEN'S VOLUNTARY SERVICE (WVS)

The WVS played an important role locally, for example in the running of the Old Barn Hall Canteen and in organising the production of clothing at Preston House (now the Preston Cross Hotel). Nationally they were involved in a wide range of valuable tasks which included running many rest centres and enquiry posts, staffing other canteens and mobile catering units as well as the billeting and welfare of evacuees and people who had been bombed out of their homes etc.

During 1943 alone a working party of the WVS operating from the house produced 1870 articles of clothing for the School for the Blind in Leatherhead and additional items for the Red Cross in Guildford. They had received three rolls of material for soldiers' pyjamas from the Bookham Committee of the Lord Lieutenant's Fund. Holborn WVS had asked the Group party to work for them using materials which they would provide as they had been bombed out of their premises. At that time, they had plenty of work in hand and were appealing for more machinists and others.

SCHOOLS

Central School in Effingham and Bookham Elementary Village School

The new Central School in Effingham (now Howard of Effingham) opened in 1939. Bookham Elementary Village School (St James) situated where the library now stands was 'relegated to the status of a Junior Mixed School for infants and children up to the age of ten'. It was originally a church school and was enlarged until its replacement in more recent years. It was the forerunner of the Dawnay School.

Southey Hall Preparatory School

In October 1941 following two bomb incidents close to hand, Southey Hall Boys' Preparatory

Southey Hall Preparatory School Photo at Southey Hall 1938

School moved to Dunsford near Exeter. The building was taken over by Canadian Military personnel and, whilst the school returned to Southey Hall after the war it was clear that considerable damage had been caused by its wartime occupants and the costs of restoring the building were beyond the resources of the school. The school eventually closed in 1954.

Manor House

The Manor House at Little Bookham was acquired by Miss H.E.Green in 1936 and she moved her existing school for girls from preparatory stage to age 18 from Mickleham.

Manor House School

Sunnyfield School

Sunnyfield School situated at the corner of Meadowside and The Park was privately run during the War years, offering an education to children between the ages of five and ten.

Spinney Preparatory Boarding School

The Spinney was a Preparatory Boarding School situated in the area now occupied by The Spinney development leading off Eastwick Drive. The school carried on throughout the war and took in a number of evacuees although a number of the pupils were moved away by their parents to a safer area of the country. Once bombing had started one room was provided with a blast wall used as a dormitory and a place of safety during the day. As Church House had become an ARP Post

The Spinney Preparatory School

the St Nicolas Girls Club moved to the gym at The Spinney for their activities. There were stories of the Canadian soldiers using the bottom of the school garden as an unguarded route in and out of Southey Hall next door.

The Strand School

The Strand School from Tulse Hill in London moved to Browns Lane in Effingham soon after the bombing commenced. The pupils were billeted around the district, many of them in Bookham. They fed at lunchtime at the canteen established in the Old Barn Hall meaning a long walk each day from Browns Lane.

Whilst school life continued everywhere as normal in many respects, the pupils were affected by the need to carry gas masks at all times, regular gas drills and the fact that at any

Browns House in Browns Lane

time at a moment's notice as soon as the wailing of the sirens was heard they might have to go to the air raid shelter or other place deemed to be safe.

D DAY AND THE CROSSWORD INCIDENT

The Daily Telegraph has always been popular for its crossword puzzle. One of the people who contributed crosswords while they were evacuated was the 54 year old headmaster of the Strand School, Leonard S Dawe (known by the boys as 'moneybags' because of his initials, LSD). Leonard Dawe was also a Lieutenant in 'B'Company of the local Home Guard.

The sites for the 6th June 1944 D-Day landings in France had long been decided as the sheltered Normandy beaches. The assault was code-named Operation Overlord by Churchill himself. A huge security blanket had been thrown over all aspects of the operation, including the place and exact date of the landings in order to maximise the element of surprise and to minimise casualties. But members of MI5, Britain's counter-espionage service while looking at the Daily Telegraph crossword in the months before the planned invasion noticed that vital codenames adopted to hide the mightiest sea-borne assault of all time appeared in a series of crosswords. All these invasion beaches had been given codenames.

In the crossword Leonard Dawes submitted for 2nd May 1944 the clue for 17 across was 'One of the US'. The answer was 'Utah'. Then on 22nd May the answer to the clue for 3 down 'Red Indian on the Missouri' was 'Omaha'. To pick a single classified code-word could be chance or coincidence but two fairly close together seemed more than that. On the 27th May 'Overlord' appeared as the answer to 11 across and on 30th May 11 across was 'This bush is the centre of nursery revolutions.' The answer was 'Mulberry.' On the 1st June the clue for 15 across was 'Britannia and he holds the same thing.' The answer was Neptune.

MI5 sprang into action - surely the crossword was being used to tip-off the Germans? Leonard Dawe was soon pulled in for the most intense questioning. Why, the officers demanded to know, without giving away the exact reason, had he chosen these five words within his crossword solutions?

'Why not?' was Dawe's indignant reply. He could choose whatever words he wanted. He eventually convinced them of his innocence.

An Old Boy later explained that at that time the senior boys frequently mixed with Canadian servicemen and these codenames were frequently banded about as the codenames of the assault points. The troops would not have had any knowledge of where the place referred to by the codename actually was. The headmaster (who incidentally was an officer in the Home Guard) often used to get the boys to help him prepare the crosswords and most likely they suggested the words to him.

Crossword 5,775 that started the panic - 17 across - 'One of the U.S.' with answer 'UTAH' one of the landing beaches for the forthcoming D-Day

No 5,775

ACROSS

1 A cause of postscripts (13)
10 Very attentive commonly (two words –3, 4)
11 A fool's weapon (7)
12 But this isn't to be bought at this shop (6)
15 Foils start thus (two words–3,3)
16 Definite (7)
17 One of the U.S. (4)
18 Achievement that the guardians of the Tower always have at heart (4)
19 Proper behaviour (7)
20 But cook has a practical use for this old weapon (4)
22 Part of one's last will and testament (4)
24 This knight of old had a fair start (7)
26 Little Samuel has got something from the pantry to make a boat (6)
27 The ceremonious tart (6)
30 Fifty fifty (7)
31 White wine (7)
33 "Intense matter"

DOWN

2 This probably has a lateen sail (7)
3 What all will be when the cease fire sounds (6)
4 Try the clue for 22 across (4)
5 Derby winner or preposition (4)
6 Systematically sorted (6)
7 When this loses its tail it doesn't grow another (7)
8 He rations the port among those who want it (13)
9 The ups and downs of business (three words –6, 3, 4)
13 Conference centre lately (7)
14 "Sleep rough" (7)
15 Lay (7)
21 Assess (7)
23 "Having drink taken" (7)
24 Many an oak-tree has this measurement (6)
25 This might make mad, sir (6)
28 This German Island sounds of alluvial origin (4)
29 The last Alice saw of the White Rabbit (4)

72

GOVERNMENT SAVINGS SCHEMES

The War Office set up schemes, for example in schools and churches, for the purchase of savings stamps to encourage the public to assist in the war effort. The Congregational Church had a membership of fifteen and raised a commendable sum of £183 in 1943. A National Savings Office was opened at Barclays Bank, then in the High Street, on two afternoons per week in order to sell savings stamps and savings certificates etc.

The savings movement was very successful in the Bookhams. In 1942 the sum of £30,988 which was raised included the figure of £15,078 in Tank Week for Bookham's Crusader Tank. In June 1943 it was announced that £17,000 was produced - enough for two Beaufighters. In 1944 'thanks to the sustained efforts of group secretaries' the 'Maintain our Men' objectives were met in the June/December period and also 'maintained its two Beaufighter aircraft during the previous winter'. Overall the sum of £40,950 was saved by Bookham's 37 Savings Groups in 1944, an increase of £5,000 on the previous year's figure. This brought Bookham's total group saving to a commendable £137,080 'since the modest opening of the campaign with seven groups in February 1940'. The fundraising results were remarkable – particularly bearing in mind the demands placed on individuals from other charitable appeals such as Aid to China, Aid to Russia, the Red Cross, the Salvation Army, Prisoner of War Fund and many more.

However, local savers were encouraged to continue their efforts.

> "There must be no faltering,"- the words of the Prime Minister Winston Churchill were relayed to the local community: "This is just the moment not to slacken ….the duty of all persons is to help the fighting man." It was said that "it is the responsibility that rests on all of us. We are all in this war and it is not yet won – it is very much ON. Vast reconstruction will follow it and continued savings out of income will be necessary to meet the cost of feeding the starving, healing the sick, rebuilding our cities. The National Savings Movement will prove of infinite value in ensuring benefits to coming generations. It is our present efforts that matter and our rising generation will, we hope, play a great part in it."

On a national basis, various savings funds were set up. Very early in the war, in 1940, 'Spitfire Funds' were established in order to raise sufficient cash to increase production of the iconic aircraft. Originally from the Ministry of Aircraft Production, also responsible for the 'Saucepans for Spitfires' campaign, the target for the purchase of a fighter was £5,000, at which point the aircraft would bear the name of the Savings Group. Other campaigns included: 'War Weapons Weeks', (1940/41), 'Warship Week' (1942), 'Wings for Victory Week' (1943) and 'Salute the Soldier Weeks' (1944). These savings campaigns raised 2.7 billion pounds 'derived from the pockets of ordinary people'. Warship Week in February 1942 came at a time when the Royal Navy was reeling from a series of blows in the Battle of the Atlantic and news had just been announced of the loss of four cruisers and sixteen destroyers in the Mediterranean. The Admiralty were desperate for replacements.

In addition to the many savings schemes in which whole communities were involved throughout the UK, individuals with considerable wealth provided the total funds to acquire for example a specific aircraft. The Hon Mrs Margaret Greville, wealthy owner of Polesden Lacey until her death in 1942, financed the manufacture of a Spitfire. This (No. P8643) was a Mark IIb manufactured at Vickers Armstrong, Castle Bromwich and fitted with a Merlin Mark II engine. The Spitfire was

A Crusader tank in action in the North African desert as funded by the Bookham Tank Week in 1942

given the name of 'MARGARET HELEN' (Mrs Greville's Christian names) and it was in active service from April 1941 until December 1944. After many raids and despite a number of accidents and incidents, it would appear that it never failed to bring its pilot home. In 1944 it was scrapped – by then battered and out of date as it had been superseded by newer and more advanced versions. At Polesden Lacey House there is a small plaque from the War Office acknowledging the gift.

It is interesting to note that many donations were also made towards the war effort by local organisations including the sum of two guineas to the Stalingrad Hospital Fund.

The plaque from the War Office at Polesden Lacey in the 'Blue Cloakroom'

LORD LIEUTENANT'S FUND

Bookham Committees for the Lord Lieutenant's Fund were formed in 1940. An Appeals Committee was to organise the raising of funds mainly for the purchase of wool. A number of local organisations staged events to raise cash for this cause. The 'Comforts Committee' co-ordinated the efforts of the working party which distributed the wool and sent 770 knitted garments for the forces in one year. An Entertainments Committee was also established when the Canadian Military arrived, a club with a canteen was set up opening for eight hours each day, all run by volunteers and much appreciated. A Christmas party was arranged and, in season, a swimming pool (probably Gilmais) was made available.

Gilmais Swimming Pool

CLUBS AND ASSOCIATIONS

With so many of the younger men and women of the villages away on war duties in various forms, many clubs would have found it hard to operate. Some of the local organisations in the villages, however, seem to have carried on their functions throughout the war years. Instead of the usual outing to the seaside no longer accessible the British Women's Total Abstinence Union (an organisation originally formed to persuade men to stop drinking) was invited to a Garden Party at the home of their President in Church Road and eighty attended. There was also a Bookham Branch of the Women's Band of Hope which had been founded in the village in 1903 in conjunction with the Congregational (now United Reform/Eastwick Road) Church and which held at least some of its meetings in the Old Barn Hall. This organisation was also a part of the Temperance Movement and had been established in the 19th century with the aim of 'saving working class children from the perils of drink' and clearly to counteract the influence of pubs and breweries. Nationally it was still very strong in the 1930s but in the post war years, its successor, Hope UK adapted to modern society and culture and aimed to reduce the UK's drink and drug problem and remained concerned with children's welfare.

It is known also that the Brownies as well as the Girl Guides and Wolf Cubs continued to function. The 1st Bookham Scouts remained very active with regular camps arranged. Meetings of the Women's Band of Hope continued to take place. Dancing classes were also organised and it is known that various events including whist drives were staged at a small hall attached to the Co-op shop on the Leatherhead Road (New Parade) as well as at the Old Barn Hall.

St Nicolas Church ran a Girls Club which ceased to operate temporarily at the outbreak of war but reopened in late 1940, meeting in the gym at the Spinney School with the main activities being 'physical culture and country dancing'. In October 1940 the Literary Society also stopped its activities for a short time. The Parish Magazine records that 'recent events make it inadvisable to push ahead with formulating a new programme. If the siren is going to obtrude itself with its present frequency and its determination after 8pm, it is, to say the least extremely doubtful whether people would wish to venture to a meeting'. A Bible Reading Fellowship (with as many as fifty members) met regularly as did the Mothers' Union.

Bookham and Fetcham Garden Society continued to hold annual shows in the war years.

Bookham Youth Club was open to all young people over the age of fifteen. Between 40 and 70 were stated to be attending such functions as: a dance at the Scout Hall, a cinema staged in the Baptist Hall and games and musical evenings at Little Bookham Hall.

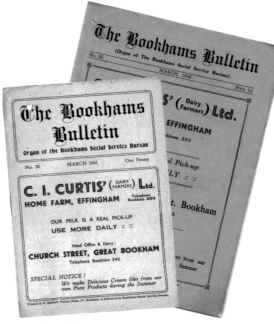

A smaller size Bookhams Bulletin was produced in 1941 to save paper

There was also a Bookham and Effingham Girls' Club which held regular meetings at the Old Barn Hall, Little Bookham Village Hall and at Effingham. Among their activities were gymnastics, badminton and handicrafts. Additionally, there were fortnightly dances jointly with senior members of the Air Training Corps at Little Bookham Village Hall.

The 2nd Mid-Surrey (Bookham) Company of the Boys Brigade gave an 'At Home' in October 1942 to parents and friends. It was pointed out however that 'the majority of the senior members who are not serving in the Forces have most of their time filled by duties of the ATC or Cadet Force and every one of the officers is a member of the Home Guard. Therefore, obviously with such compelling obligations, the entertainment could not be expected to show the company's usual display standard, but the right spirit was there and there was no lack of Boys Brigade humour'. In 1940 the Boys Brigade played Bookham Scouts at cricket.

Bookham Choral Society was in 1941 in its 11th season but operating with a reduced membership 'as evening activities were considered inadvisable' for a time.

In many other respects life went on as usual. For instance, in August 1942 the Congregational Church took some children to Chessington Zoo and 'a very happy tea party followed'.

There was encouragement to arrange local entertainment and in fact, in May 1942, all local councils including Leatherhead received a request from the Ministry of Health to this end, so as to avoid residents travelling too far. However, the Bookham Branch of the Amalgamated Engineering Union had written to protest that the Council had not agreed to co-operate.

As is the case today, the Bookhams Bulletin continued to inform residents about activities of the local clubs. In those days, however, the Bulletins were produced by the Bookham Social Service Bureau. From Issue 29 in December 1940, due to restrictions on the supply of paper, the publication was much reduced in size (from approximately quarto to approximately A5). The Bulletins were used also to disseminate official Government and Local Council information.

WOMEN'S INSTITUTES

Women's Institutes played a significant part in the life of the country particularly in rural areas during the war. Bookham Afternoon WI, an organisation which sadly ceased to exist in recent years (although three other local WIs still function) was no exception. Formed in 1929 they had previously held meetings at Church House but when this was taken over as an ARP Post they moved to 'The Croft' in Church Road and subsequently to the Congregational Hall due to an increase in the numbers attending.

Meetings always commenced with the singing of 'Jerusalem' and ended with the National Anthem. The war was never far from their minds; in January 1943 the President, Mrs Newman, opened the meeting by wishing the members 'a Happy New Year as possible under existing conditions', adding 'although the news is heartening, we must not forget the submarine menace and to make the utmost use of potatoes and use less bread.' One assumes that this alludes to the shortage of imported grain due to raids on shipping.

One visiting speaker in November 1942 on 'Today and Tomorrow' said: 'housing should not only be lovely to look at but labour saving, and women should voice their opinions on new housing schemes'. "Children,", she said, "are the future citizens and should be trained for future utility." The speaker also advised members 'not to spend but lend what they saved for their country'.

Amongst the WI's Groups were: the Drama Group, the Choir ('depleted at one stage due to war work'), a Concert Party known as 'The Versatile Victorians' formed in 1938 and which entertained people in Bookham and area during the war years, a Produce Guild, a Public Affairs Group, and a Debating Club.

Food restrictions of course affected their meetings and, as early as July 1939, it had been stated that 'as the time had come for the surrender of tea and sugar licences, it had been agreed that each member should bring to the meetings a teaspoon each of tea and sugar' and later eight members were each asked to bring to the meetings a tin of milk.

The WI assisted in many ways either directly or indirectly in the war effort. Some examples are:

- In January 1943 they were thanked for providing rabbit skins, stretched and dried, urgently required for Mrs Churchill's Russian Fund

- Eggs were provided to Leatherhead Hospital in April each year (usually between ten and twenty dozen)

- Vegetable seeds were sold – at one point at between 1s 5d and 3s 9d per packet with tomatoes at 6d per packet

- The Savings Group was very active with up to fifty members in support of such schemes as the Spitfire Fund, Salute the Soldier and War Weapons Fund. In April 1943 £374 was raised for the Wings for Victory week against a target of £200, the main fundraising events being a Whist Drive and a combined concert by the Drama Group and the Choir. Previously prizes of silver spoons were given at the meetings but this was changed to Savings Stamps in wartime.

- Vouchers were distributed to the needy in the Bookhams prior to Christmas

- Assistance was given to the Ministry of Information in typing and in cycling to deliver messages around the villages

- The bottling of fruit and jam making

- Help provided at the 'Soldier's Canteen'

- Garments made and sent to the Armed Forces

- In January 1943 the proceeds of items sold at a WI stall were sent through the Red Cross 'aiming to help prisoners of war' and members were asked to submit names of local men known to be prisoners at that time

- In January 1945 members of the WI were asked to provide hospitality to Dutch children coming to this country

PUBLIC SERVICE MEETINGS

Public Service Meetings were also held and in August 1942 one such meeting was convened when a local resident informed a well attended gathering that in the event of an invasion a triumvirate would be set up with himself, Lt N of the Home Guard and 'Sgt G'. of the police as members. The police would give instructions as to local leaders. Lt N said the main task of the public was to keep out of the way of the military. 'Don't leave the area to go to work'.

'Sgt G' addressed the meeting, reading his speech word for word very deliberately: "Everyone should obey the police who may be distinguished from Fifth Columnists by their warrant card with photo, but at such a time you would be unlikely to have an opportunity to check a constable's bona fides."

The report comments that this raised the biggest laugh of the evening. Later comments included 'Fancy having that man ('Sgt G') giving orders. Why choose the most unpopular man in the district?'

SCRAP METAL

In March 1942 there was a public announcement that scrap iron, for example iron railings was then being collected in three counties and it would be Surrey's turn soon. Residents were encouraged to save all they could, not only iron but paper, rags, bottles and tins, all of which were needed.

TRANSPORT

A bus service (408) operated to Croydon and there were other local services. With the lack of petrol and cars there was greater reliance on public transport and the comment has been made recently that the train services in the wartime were 'better than those available today'. Bookham Station was opened by the London and Western Railway Co in 1885 (in a location well away from the village centres - apparently on the insistence of the then local Lords of the Manor). The line was electrified in 1925 soon after the creation of the Southern Railway in 1923. A public telephone line was not installed at the station until 1938!

As the war neared its end in 1945, the main railway companies issued a Public Mobility Notice which stated: 'The railway have preserved public mobility even through the whole huge mass of war, transport has been their responsibility. Without the railways, there would be no family visits, no holiday travel and no business trips. Once the nation's war job is done, the railways will set about restoring all the comfort, speed and luxury of peace time travelling'.

BLACKOUT OFFENCES

The regulations were strictly enforced and the Dorking Advertiser reported the following transgressions.

Black-out Offence - At Epsom Police Court on Thursday, Marion Greenley, of Langdale End, Crabtree Road, Great Bookham, was fined £2 for allowing a light to be visible during black-out hours and Kate Blanche McGruther, of Danby Croft, Great Bookham was fined £1 for a like offence. (July 1940)

Lights in the Black-out - After pleading that at the time she was giving a birthday party for three evacuees billeted with her, Mrs Emily Stone, of Walmer Cottage, School-lane, Great Bookham was fined £2 by the Epsom Bench on Monday for allowing a light to be visible from her premises during black-out hours. It was stated that the light was seen while a raid warning was in progress. (October 1940)

Lights in the Black-out - Summoned at Epsom Petty Sessions on Thursday of last week for allowing a light to be visible from his premises during black-out hours, Percy Shoesmith, Oakdene, Oakdene Road, Little Bookham was fined 30s. (November 1940)

LIGHTS IN THE BLACK-OUT.—Harry Ruddock, manager of the Co-operative Stores, Great Bookham, was summoned at Epsom Petty Sessions on Thursday for allowing a light to be shown from the Co-operative Stores during black-out hours. He pleaded guilty. A police officer stated the premises were locked up at the time and he had to force an entry in order to put out a 200-watt electric bulb. Defendant told the Bench he had the light on in daylight and forgot to switch it off. A fine of £3 was imposed. — Mrs. Mabel Annie Niland, Kinwarton, Commonside, Fetcham, was fined £2 at the same Court for a similar offence.

Lights in the Black-out - Mrs. Kate Blanch McGruther of Danby Croft, Leatherhead-road (sic), Great Bookham was summoned at Epsom Petty Sessions on Monday for allowing a light to be visible from her premises during the black-out hours. PC Beale proved the case and defendant asked the Bench, "Why was it her place was watched night after night when other lights were always showing." She was fined £2 with 16s costs. (November 1940)

Lights in the Black-out - At Epsom Petty Sessions Leonard Cyril Weeden of Stanmuir, Keswick Road, Great Bookham who told the Bench that he was an air raid warden was summoned for a similar offence. PC Beale stated that light was showing from an attic window at 1.30am while the occupants of the house were sleeping in a shelter at the bottom of the garden. A fine of £2 was imposed.

On a farm in Little Bookham - 'all the windows in their buildings had to be painted black so that light used during milking times could not be observed.'

IMPACT ON THE LOCAL POPULATION

In assessing the effect that the war had on the local population it is interesting that residents who were interviewed and were all quite young at the time had such a range of experiences which have remained with them for over seventy years. One commented, "As a child it was very bewildering and I did not really understand it because the worst part was over by the time I was eight or nine years of age. It was a time of caution and restriction. I knew food was getting short and, I think, clothes as well." Some young residents at the time expressed a feeling of excitement despite the seriousness of the situation. Another commented, "If anything the war brought people together" and that there was a feeling of camaraderie.

Others recall a mix of memories:

- The army convoys passing through

- The sound of bombs and, later the noise of doodlebugs

- The throbbing sound of German aircraft

- The sight of 'dog fights' overhead

- The air raid sirens

- Watching the searchlights being operated from local sites

- The ill-lit, cold and damp school air raid shelter

- At home, sheltering in a Morrison Shelter or merely hiding under the kitchen table during an enemy raid

- The spectacular, if worrying, distant view from the Leatherhead/Guildford Road of the bombing in London and the glow in the sky, particularly during the 'Blitz'

- Listening to the stirring speeches on the wireless by Winston Churchill and despite his difficulties, by King George VI

- The sight of Italian POW's playing football at the recreation ground

- Carrying gas masks to school in their cardboard boxes and the regular gas drill

- Walking in a 'crocodile' from Bookham School for lunch at the Old Barn Hall, on one occasion accompanied by Canadian soldiers wearing kilts and playing a pipe band,

- The ability to find good firework material, using cordite out of shells and percussion caps from .303 bullets to set them off

- Collecting shrapnel and fins from exploded bombs

- The Canadian servicemen, including a grand Christmas party to which all the children in the village were invited

With so many men away on essential duties more women undertook jobs that previously had been

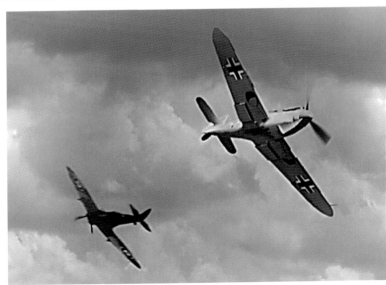

A Battle of Britain dogfight with a Spitfire on the tail of a Messerschmidt 109

regarded as male occupations. Children stayed at their local school until they moved to the Central School either at Leatherhead or Effingham. One local resident who when she left Leatherhead School aged fourteen had employment at Pixham Court in Dorking and cycled the seven miles there each day.

PRISONERS OF WAR (POWS)

Very little seems to have been reported about POWs in Bookham but it is recorded that after the successful North African campaign many German POWs were to be seen working on the land. There were, it would appear several POW camps in the general area - specific mention is made of a camp in Merrow for which there is a 1:500 scale diagram in the records in Woking. The Dorking Grey Stone Lime Co certainly employed Italian POWs who were paid the same rate as unskilled British labour. The mill which was situated where Mill Close in Church Road is today is also believed to have had Italian POWs working there.

Chapter 6

THE CANADIAN ARMY IN BOOKHAM

ROYAL CANADIAN ARTILLERY

During the early part of WW II the entire County of Surrey was transformed by the arrival of numerous Canadian army units, and Bookham did not escape this friendly invasion. The evacuation of Southey Hall School in 1940 left the house and grounds available for alternative use. The 4th Battalion of the Royal Canadian Engineers were stationed at the house from 17th May 1942 for an unknown period and there is no record of their activities during their stay. On the 19th August 1942 the 4th Medium Regiment of the Royal Canadian Artillery from Canada arrived there via Liverpool. It is noted that, of the 27 officers listed in the regiment, 24 had French-Canadian surnames. Captain Sevigny of the regiment was reported to have said on arrival: "Can you imagine being paid to live here?" even though the unit that preceded it had apparently left it in a state of extreme disrepair. He appeared fascinated by the countryside, the history and the location's proximity to London.

The Canadians soon realised that they were in a war zone when on 27th August the Order of the Day decreed: 'In the event of air-raids all personnel should seek shelter under trees, or if not possible, lie face down and avoid looking skywards.' Bookham ARP was responsible for the local air-raid siren and the 'All Clear' was repeated by the regiment's own siren. The troops were also given strict security instructions.

Major-General Vanier (later Governor-General of Canada) and other officers

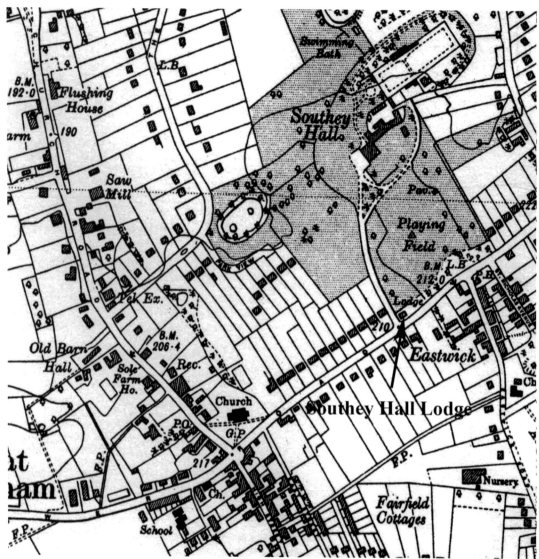

Map showing Southey Hall. From the Lodge gates which still stand at 182A Lower Road you can see the drive to the Hall. Prewar it was a school and the playing fields are marked.

On 26th August two six inch howitzers arrived on loan, and for two weeks, 12 hours per day they were used in training by the very inexperienced gunners. The next day saw the arrival of a British artillery officer, Captain Hudson to assist in this training.

On 1st September the regiment received a staff car, six jeeps, a 5½ ton and two three-ton trucks, still well below the regimental strength of 16 guns, 100 vehicles and 32 motorcycles. More howitzers arrived on 9th September and on that day Major Archer and Lieutenant Laplante attended the funeral of the Duke of Kent who had been killed on the 25th August in Scotland when the Sunderland Flying Boat in which he was flying to Iceland crashed on its way to meet senior members of the US military.

(Left) Major Maurice Archer, Col Panet, Major Réal Gagnon and Capt Rolande Codère
(Right) Major Gagnon and Col Panet

An entertainments officer was soon appointed and visits to the Tower of London and Windsor Castle were arranged. Bingo sessions were also arranged but in spite of these distractions Leatherhead still seemed to be more attractive. London Transport asked the Canadians to cooperate to avoid overcrowding the buses into the town especially in the evenings.

A Baptist Church report mentioned that 'Bookham and the surrounding countryside were 'invaded' by the Canadians' described as although 'big, rough and kindly ... we were glad to have them and often entertained them in our hall'.

In 1942 a framed copy of an etching of St Nicolas Church was presented to the Canadians by the Rector and subsequently a letter was received from the Commanding Officer expressing their appreciation for the use of the church and the friendly attitude shown to them by the people of Great Bookham.

At the beginning of October the first official inspection was held by British and Canadian artillery officers. This was followed by an exercise in which the entire regiment went in convoy to Tattenham Corner where there was a vehicle exhibition - the real purpose of the exercise being to assess their mobility. Such was the state of their unreadiness, and with the winding roads slowing the convoy down, some 500 men accompanied by trucks and wagons and motorcycle escorts managed to get lost during the seven mile journey and arrived just before the exhibition closed.

Two days later the first dance was held at Southey Court and was attended by Major General Roberts who had commanded the ill fated raid on 19th August 1942 when the allied command had given the Canadians the almost impossible task of establishing a beachhead against a well-fortified enemy at Dieppe.

In November the Canadians opened their own School of Artillery at Larkhill on Salisbury Plain where eventually all Bookham officers attended regular classes. With the advent of the 1942 winter roads around Southey Hall became increasingly impassable and a British officer was brought in to sort out the traffic problems. On 19th December the entire regiment proceeded to Alfriston near Brighton and by that evening were ready to go into action the next day. It was found however that the proposed quantity of cordite to be used would be too great for the firing area and not a shell was fired.

On 17th January 1943 in spite of a two-hour air-raid alert in Bookham the regiment set off for a firing range in North Wales where the inexperienced gunners managed to achieve remarkable accuracy. Morale was reported to be excellent. On returning to Bookham new 5½ inch guns replaced the outdated howitzers and were tested at Alfriston and the regiment participated in firing exercises all over England.

Back in Bookham June and July 1943 were relatively calm. Major-General Vanier (later Governor General of Canada) made an official visit on 16th June and this was followed a few days later by a dance and a game of softball between officers and a team of London-based Canadian Womens Army Corps.

In October 1943 the whole regiment moved to Caterham and eventually landed in Normandy on 10th July 1944.

ROYAL CANADIAN ENGINEERS

The next Canadian units to be located in Southey Hall might be regarded as less belligerent than their predecessors. The 3rd Field Survey Company (FSC), Royal Canadian Engineers (RCE), who were engaged in map making for such things as training purposes and artillery targeting had arrived in England in February 1940 and, after a number of moves came to Southey Hall from Wakehurst Place in Sussex in late March 1944. During their time in Bookham a section was attached to No 2 Canadian corps in Dover. Many of the men had fond memories of the Crown Public House where one of the locals led the singing on the piano in return for liquid refreshment. The son of the pianist, Henry Griffiths who was also the organist and Choir Master at St Nicolas Church remembers going in to the Old Crown one evening to find that his father had seventeen pints lined up on the piano. He told us he was happy to help his father deal with the accumulation! They also recalled the advent of V1 flying bombs (doodlebugs) which started to pass over the area in June.

In July the company was divided into two Flights, the first moving to Gosport via Winchester before sailing to France on 28th July. The second Flight moved on 2nd July to Tilbury and embarked for France on 31st July.

Another Field Survey Company, No 4, also came to Bookham at the end of March 1944 and were in close proximity to 2 and 3 Companies. This particular company was reported to have moved in with 'outdoor plumbing facilities, chicken pens and a pigsty etc' Bookham was considered to 'look very good: pubs close at hand, people seem very friendly, train service not too bad'. During April visits were made by personnel from 83 Squadron RAF, and two more good pubs, The Bell and The Rising Sun in Fetcham were discovered and rated as good.

Canadian 1st and 2nd Flight

Back row, (left to right)—Spr Oldfield, L. A., Spr Slade, W. T., Spr Oliver, W. D., Spr Demars, E., Spr Baker, J. R., L/Cpl Ambrose, B. W., Spr Hickey, W. A., Spr Tomlinson, A. E., Spr Kline, R. L., Spr Marshall, G., Cpl O'Toole, J. E., Spr Scrimshaw, C., Spr Wilson, W. D., Spr Androschuk, G., L/Cpl Downing, H. A., L/Cpl Weiss, C. F., Spr Lovatt, J. K., Spr Nickorak, N., L/Cpl Blood, R. M. *Fourth row*—Spr Cundy, P. M., Spr Allen, D. R., Spr Pruden, Spr Dwyer, J. C., Spr Lamb, C. C., Spr Rohaly, J., Spr Cassidy, E. J., Spr Thomson, J. L., Spr Neil, J. Y., Spr Hynes, J. W., Spr Comley, E. G., Spr Kenney, G., L/Cpl Briggs, F. C. V., Spr Hoffer, H., L/Cpl Corscadden, L. A., Spr Watson, J. C., Spr Simpson, J. D., Spr Hollinger, C., Spr Andrews, C. W., Spr McLeod, D. *Third row*—Cpl Jemmett, F. J. E., Cpl Dennahower, G. A., L/Sgt Quinn, W. G., Sgt Austin, W. J., Sgt Large, J. A., CSM Lebeau, J. E., Lt Turner, E. S., Maj Wass, L. F., Lt Dadson, S. F., CQMS Kerrison, H. E., L/Sgt Bateman, E. R., L/Sgt Boschi, G. P., Cpl Dupuis, J. C. M. R., Cpl Robertson, W. J., Cpl Brown, R. M., L/Cpl Frith, T. J., Cpl Strong, K. C. *Second row*— L/Sgt Wood, M. F., L/Cpl McDonald, J. A., Spr Lavers, R. W., Spr Clarke, E. H., Spr Smith, H. V., Spr Gunderson, R. C., Spr Gallant, J. R., Spr Gilley, K. N., Spr Lacombe, P., Spr Bruce, G. H., Spr Swaffield, A. E., Spr Norris, J. E., Spr Fouchard, G. W., Spr Brown, F. W., Spr Watkins, H. H. *Front row*—Spr McDougall, A. A., Spr Smith, Spr Cutts, H. P., Spr Miller, J. S., Spr Asselin, A., Spr Rhyno, G. A., Spr Kerr, J. I., Spr Magwood, V. E., Spr Shewchuk, W., Spr Estabrooks, G. A.

Back row, left to right)—Spr Phillimore, T. C., Spr Toutloff, I. G., Spr Gilbert, E. G., Spr Campbell, A. M., Spr Perkins, E. W., Spr Prest, V. F., Spr Young, G. F., Spr Collins, W. C., Spr Shillington, R. J., Spr Miller, H., Spr Apland, H. G. Spr Musselwhite, A. L., Spr Arpin, J. E., Spr Polistac, W. *Third row*—Spr Smalley, G. W., Spr Ambrose, B. W., Spr Elwood, C. C., Spr Gardham, F. G., Spr Kemp, A. W., Spr Finer, W., Spr Crawford, M. D., L/Cpl Waller P. de W., Spr Hebert, R. H., Spr Edison, R. A., Spr Gilbert, T. H., L/Cpl Grimble, R. G., Spr Duggan, J. C., Spr Watt, H. M., L/Cpl Carder, A. W., L/Cpl Starkman, H., Spr Manson, W. D., Spr St Amand, R. A. Spr Carson, S., Spr Harris, H. A., Spr Scrimshaw, C. *Second row*—Spr Bragg, K. O., Spr Hurd, H. E., L/Sgt Hogg, G. J., Sgt McNeely, C. E., L/Sgt Thauberger, P. W., L/Sgt Bassett, J., Sgt Spearman, G. E., L/Sgt Disher, K., Lt Gill, H. C. W., Capt J. A. Thornton, Lt R. C .Richards, Cpl Barnes, R. G., Cpl Read, G., Cpl Stein, T. M., L/Cpl Robertson, W. J., Spr Hollinger, W., Spr Stafford, W. H., Spr Youngs, J. M., Spr Higney, R. B. *First row*—Spr Stewart, H. N., Spr Borley, J. C., Spr Cairncross, J. D., Spr Benwood, J., Spr Bowden, J., Spr Hamel, A., Spr Brooks, D. E., Spr Reynolds, J. C., Spr Chapman, A. E., Spr Johnston, H. R., Spr Creagen, H. E., Spr Moore, J. M., Spr Johnson, A. A., Spr Sweet, J., Spr Yeo, C. W.

All vehicles were now being waterproofed in readiness for Normandy and their baseball team vied with those from 2 and 3 Companies for the use of the field. In May it was reported that 'hospitality is being offered to us everywhere round here'. One Sapper 'dropped into the local hop at Fetcham Village Hall the other evening and demonstrated a few new steps to everyone present'. On 2nd June he 'spent one evening walking over the fields to Mickleham to a fine pub there, The Running Horses'.

On 17th June the General Officer Commanding (GOC) visited and nightly visits from V1s were experienced, with a very good view obtained from Southey Hall roof as they went over. Also in that month they participated in the Leatherhead 'Salute the Soldier Week'. July and August were spent in mapping exercises of the French coast, and on 12th August they started packing with a big Company farewell dance held in the Hall before leaving for Normandy where they arrived on 25th August.

On the 5th July 1945 the 10th Canadian Repatriation Depot opened, one of eleven in Surrey and Hampshire. It closed down on 28th January 1946 by which time most of the Canadians had returned home. When the school returned from Devon at the end of the war they found Southey Hall in a state of utter disrepair and were forced to close in 1954. The only remains now are the gateposts at the entrance to 182A Lower Road.

There are now few anecdotal stories remaining about the Canadians' stay in Bookham. The evacuee from New Eltham reckoned that the Canadians were great guys getting them involved in all manner of things especially boxing tournaments when they would put a couple of kids in the ring wearing huge pillow gloves competing as 'paperweights' or 'dustweights'.

As they grew older, more inquisitive and cheekier some of the youngsters would hide in the overgrown grass and weeds in the grounds of the old Victoria Hotel and wait for a soldier to bring one of the village maidens into the gardens for some 'hanky panky'. Once they had got settled into the 'old routine' the boys would leap up, dance around them like dervishes and shout, whoop and holler. They would then run 'like hell' never to be caught although there were a few close calls depending on the state of undress. Also there were inevitability some other liaisons which caused clear concern to parents worrying about their daughters. As one of those interviewed told us, "My Dad said if you come home with 'trouble' you can take 'trouble' away with you." She added, "at the time I didn't know what he meant, but I do now!"

The Lloyds Bank building is reputed to have been the site of the Canadian Army Post Office and the RCE converted The Park from a track into a road.

YOUNG STREET

Bookham residents of a certain age usually associate the Canadians with the building of Young Street. which had already been projected during peacetime but had to be postponed on the outbreak of war. In 1940 however there was an urgent need for the speeding-up of military traffic and to improve the movement of mobile reserves in the event of invasion. Following the receipt of the necessary go-ahead from the Ministry of War Transport, 2nd Road Construction Company RCE with its HQ in

Oxshott where the brickwork site was used as a workshop and equipment park moved in with the latest US road building machinery having completed similar works at Reigate and Redhill. Many of the large houses in Stoke D'Abernon and Cobham were requisitioned to accomodate the men.

The idea was to link the two main roads running south and west from Leatherhead with a 22ft. concrete carriageway 1¼ miles in length. The subsoil conditions consisted mainly of chalk overlaid with silty clay - dusty in dry weather and sticky when wet. There were numerous flints in the chalk which played havoc with tyres and scraper blades and work was often interrupted with machines bogged down in the rain-affected ground. The railway had to be underpassed and the River Mole frequently overtopped its banks. Nevertheless the entire construction was completed in the summer of 1941 and officially opened by the Prime Minister of Canada, Mackenzie King on 28th August 1941.

The opening of Young Street by the Prime Minister of Canada, William Lyon Mackenzie King on 28th August 1941

It is worth mentioning that the construction of roads such as this helped to bring the bulldozer into prominence as an essential item of military equipment. During the grading of Young Street a number of tank trials were made at the roadside and these in part led to the development of the armoured bulldozer which was later to play such an important part in Sicily, Italy and later in the Normandy landings.

The building of Young Street is commemorated on a plaque at the Givons Grove Roundabout and there is a Canadian Peace memorial by the access road to Bocketts Farm.

The Young Street Plaque - Givons
Grove
The Plaque reads:

'YOUNG ST
Built by a Company of Royal
Canadian Engineers and named
after the Commanding Officer.
This road was opened on 28th day
of August 1941 by the Rt Hon Wm
Lyon Mackenzie King, Prime
Minister of Canada.'

Peace Memorial Plaque at the top of Young
Street by the access road to Bockett's Farm

FRIENDSHIP (MAPLE) TREE AND PLAQUE

During their stay at Southey Hall the Canadians planted two trees - a red-leafed Canadian maple and green-leafed English maple as a symbol of the friendship between the two countries. The two trees have fused together over time and the Friendship Tree as it is now known, has become one. In spring one half of the tree blooms red leaves, the other green.

In October 2005 some sixty years after the Canadians had left Bookham a plaque was unveiled at 5 Eastwick Park Avenue close to where Southey Hall once stood. The historic memorial was unveiled by Ron Smith, a local historian who recalled the activities of the Canadians in the area during the war.

The Plaque that was unveiled in 2005

Standing under the Friendship Maple Tree at the Remembrance Day Gathering 2010

Chapter 7

THE WAR IS OVER

Once the war ended there was an overwhelming feeling of relief in the community followed by victory celebrations.

VE DAY - VICTORY IN EUROPE

Bookham celebrated the end of the War in style. There was a spontaneous party outside 'The Old Crown' to mark VE (Victory in Europe) Day on 8th May 1945. The pianist from the pub, George Shepherd played the piano accordion and there was singing and impromptu dancing. An armchair apparently was tossed onto a bonfire which had been lit on the crossroads and a vehicle caught fire. Some say this was a car, others, more romantically a haywain! It was reported that the helmet of the local policeman was knocked off and thrown down the manhole whose cover had been damaged by the fire. Other, more organised celebrations took place later. On 19th May children from the Fairfield Housing Estate were entertained to a party on the Green (the Fairfield) by Mrs Ayres and Mrs Francis. Tea was followed by dancing, games and a bonfire. On the same day a family party was given in the Co-operative Hall to welcome home a returning Prisoner of War, Walter Gurr. There was a Village Fete in Little Bookham on Saturday 26th May and on the following two Saturdays other children from the Village were entertained at parties in both the Baptist Church Hall and the Co-operative Hall.

Cuttings from the Surrey Advertiser:

'A 'welcome home' family party was given in the Co-operative hall to celebrate the return of Walter Gurr, son of Mrs Lidbitter, Fairfield Cottages, after 3½ years as a POW in Italy and Germany.'

'Victory Party organised by Mrs Ayres and Mrs Francis given to 150 adults and children from Fairfield Cottages and Flint Cottages. Tables were laid in Fairfield for a substantial tea followed by conjuring entertainment. Pony rides were also given.' (May 1945)

'On Saturday Little Bookham celebrated VE Day with a village fete. A substantial tea was followed by races on the village green organised by D Longhurst and R V Williams. B Longhurst created much fun as a clown. Each child received 1s 6d. Children helped collect materials for a bonfire which was surmounted by an effigy of Hitler. Dancing and singing tool place round the fire and there were fireworks. Later the adults gathered for dancing and singing in the Village Hall.' (26th May 1945)

'Children, numbering 80 from High Street, Church Road, Lower Road and School Lane were given a victory fete with tea, sports and entertainment organised by Mrs Burberry in the Baptist Hall.' (2nd June 1945)

'Children from Howard Road, Dawnay Road and Dorking Road, numbering 80, were given

VE Day celebrations at Little Bookham - notice the effigy of Hitler at the top of the post

a victory party last Wednesday in the Co-operative Hall. Entertainment with Punch and Judy, conjuring and sports on the recreation ground was followed by singing and dancing.' (9th June 1945)

VJ DAY - VICTORY OVER JAPAN

VJ Day (15th August) was celebrated in similar style. There were parties in August and September in which Canadian troops took part. The final celebratory events took place in October organised by the Peace Celebrations Committee preceded by an outing to Littlehampton on Friday 29th September. At a gathering on Bookham Recreation Ground in Dorking Road tea was served in a marquee for 50 adults over the age of 60 and 600 children. There was also a tug-of-war and a wrestling and boxing exhibition put on by the Canadians. The day - which was styled 'Young People's Day' by the Chairman of Leatherhead Urban Council - finished with a torchlight procession and bonfire. A 'Welcome Home' supper also took place at the Baptist Church in October 1946 when either a Baptist Church hymnal or a Welcome Home book was presented to each of the returning service men or women.

Cuttings from the Surrey Advertiser

'10th Canadian Repatriation Depot helped at a grand gala and 'water follies' at Gilmais Pool.' (25th August 1945)

'Children from The Park and Meadowside enjoyed a victory party in the Old Barn Hall on Saturday organised by Mrs Hunter and aided by Mrs Bently and Mrs Shelton. Miss Gott played the piano. There were games and conjuring and each child was given a victory beaker. Parent and friends gathered in the evening at Sunnyfields, The Park for dancing , games and coffee.' (1st September 1945)

'Great and Little Bookham residents are combining on 28th and 29th September. Friday will be devoted to a children's outing and on Saturday there will be a fete for the two villages. Canadians stationed at Southey Hall will contribute to the entertainment and the Home Guard and Civil Defence personnel are taking part. Contributions in money and in kind are coming in on a generous scale as the result of a house-to-house collection.' (15th September 1945)

'The Canadian pipe band attended the wedding on Thursday last of Miss Cicely Buckland and Bdr Orville J Cochraine of the Royal Canadian Artillery at the Bookham Baptist Church.'

'The Bookham Recreation Ground was the scene for the programme arranged by the Peace celebrations Committee. The previous day (29th Sept) 300 children and 70 adults went to Littlehampton where the sun shone and the children had a happy time. Proceedings opened on Saturday with a fancy dress parade, headed by the Boys Brigade Band, in which there were nearly 200 entrants. Mr Murrells (chairman of Leatherhead Urban District Council) opened the fete saying it was 'Young People's Day'. The older people had had their celebrations and now it was felt that they wanted to return to those things which the children had missed during the war. Tea was served to 600 children and 50 adults over 60 years of age in a marquee. The Home Guard tug-of-war team beat the Civil Defence team and the Great Bookham team beat that of Little Bookham. Canadian soldiers staged a boxing and wrestling exhibition and wholeheartedly supported the event. A torchlight procession in which over 100 took part was followed by the lighting of a huge bonfire surmounted by an effigy. A committee under the chairmanship of P J Hewitt (headmaster of Effingham Central School) with R Andrews (Treasurer) and Mrs Carter (Secretary) carried out the arrangements.' (6th October 1945)

The District Rep for the Surrey Advertiser who covered The Bookhams was Miss E Jones, Angleside, 11 Church Road.

BACK TO PEACETIME

The demobilisation of the armed forces began in June 1945 within six weeks of VE day and in the following eighteen months all kinds of personal challenges were experienced by returning service men and women on their return to civilian life. Britain had undergone six years of bombardment and blockade and there was a shortage of many of the basic essentials of living, including food, clothing and housing. An austere economic climate prevailed and resources were not available to expand food production and food imports. Husbands and wives also had to adjust to living together again after many years apart. One indicator of the social problems was the postwar UK divorce rate with over 60,000 applications in 1947 alone, a figure that was not reached again until the 1960s.

Life very slowly returned to some normality although there were still many reminders of the restrictions imposed during the war with rationing. Rationing continued after the end of the war for some nine years with some aspects becoming even stricter. Bread, which had been reduced in quality during the war but not formally controlled was rationed from 1946 to 1948; potato rationing began in 1947. Eventually petrol rationing ended in 1950. Sweet rationing ended in 1953 and sugar rationing later that year. The end of all food rationing did not come until 4th July 1954 with meat the last to become freely available again.

Church House which had been sequestrated during the war had been one of the main venues for social activities prior to 1939 and although the church submitted an application for desequestration once the war was over it was another year before it was returned to the parish.

After the end of the war and with demobilisation, compulsory National Service was introduced for men aged 17 and above initially for a period of eighteen months which was later extended to two years to be followed by a further three year term as a Reservist. Compulsory National Service did not end until the end of 1960 some fifteen years after the war ended.

Postscript

What are our overall impressions and conclusions of what it was like to be living in The Bookhams during the War years?

Our main impression is that life carried on as normally as it could wherever possible. Clubs and Societies remained active and the Churches continued to have an important presence. Local people became as self sufficient as they were able. Saving, self-help and mutual support were significant features. There was a general feeling that 'if anything the War brought people together'. Most parents and grandparents were still very mindful of the horrors of the 1914-18 conflict but many youngsters saw it as a time of general excitement.

It was fortunate that most of the real horrors of war passed the Bookhams by. Nobody was killed in the village itself as the result of enemy action although at least one youngster was killed by a bomb in Leatherhead. There were, regrettably, inevitably service casualties, but they were not on the scale of those in the First World War from what was then a much smaller community.

The general feeling in the locality is probably well summed-up in the words of a person who was a local resident at the time: 'But the Blitz spirit wasn't just to be found in the cities. Its tentacles spread the length and breadth of Britain, infusing towns and villages with renewed vigour. Here in Bookham it was well and truly alive and kicking. Us villagers were the backbone of Britain.'

In short 'The Bookhams in the War' was essentially - to borrow a theme from 'The Archers' - a 'day to day story of everyday folk'.

Michael Anderson, Project Leader

APPENDIX A
BOOKHAM BUSINESSES IN 1939

HIGH STREET

Name	Nature of Business	Location
The Crown, F Wigley	Family & Commercial Hotel	The Old Crown
Donaldsons	Men's & Boy's Outfitters	9, Princess Alice Hospice
J Davies	Hairdresser	13
Barclays Bank	Bank (part time)	15
A C Annetts	Builders	17A, Brackenbury
Alexander Stent	Barber	Passage next to Cascade Too
F Allman	Estate Agent	Buildings south of passage
Jackson's Graneries	Corn Dealer	Buildings south of passage
A Lewer	Chimney Sweep	Buildings south of passage
M A Perry	Drapery & Millinery	27 Elio Barbers
Page Bros / Drakes	Grocers	31, Salon 31
W R Hewlins	Chemist & Druggist	35, Childrens Trust
H Absalom	Sweet Shop	37, Harts
Absalom's Stores	Groceries & Hardware	39, Fosters, Dry Cleaners
A Lutman	Butcher	45, Beverley Floral Designs
S Worral & Sons	Butcher	Formerly Roberts
Mrs E Oliver	Confectioner	unknown
Freemen Marskell	Cycle Engineer	unknown
Lloyds Bank	Bank	2, Lloyds Bank
M W Hanson	Baker & Confectioner	6, Pearces Bakery
Walker Smith	Grocer	8, Co-op (Somerfield)
J Stemp & Sons	Saddlers, Boot & Shoe Repairs	Royal Oak car park
Royal Oak	Public House	Royal Oak
Victoria Hotel		32, Fine Fettle & Henshaws Estate Agents

CHURCH ROAD

Name	Nature of Business	Location
Womens Voluntary Service (WVS)	Canteen for troops	Corner House, Patrick Gardner

Birch & Gott	Electrical Engineers/Cyclists	9, Gothic House, Donners Optician
Post Office	Post Office	11, Post Office
S Madge	Butcher	25, Howard Electrical
Old Barn Hall	Registrar of Births & Deaths	Old Barn Hall
J H Irwin	Provisions, Hardware Drapery	Bardolin House
Ford's	Estate Agent	24, Mimi's Tea Room
W H LeGrove	Lending Library	24, Mimi's Tea Room
Frances	Ladies Outfitter	30, Patchwork
A Longhurst	Landscape Gardener	Park Lodge Area
C I Curtis	Dairy	40, Lincoln Joyce Art Gallery
E A Hayter	Newsagent	42, Newsagent
O Higby	Builder	Worsted House
F C Bellows	Hardware	Rothwell House
H Ranger	Fishmonger	Cochrane House
Rangers	Coal & Coke Sales	Sweet Pea building
H Allen	Corn Dealer	The Mill building
F N Goodhew	Motor Body Builders	near Millside Court
J Harvey Prince	Optician	unknown
Gillett Stephen	New Atlas Works, Aircraft parts	Bookham Industrial Estate
Stanley Bellows	Confectioner	Station Yard

LEATHERHEAD ROAD

Name	Nature of Business	Location
F Barford	Victory Press	unknown
MacDonald	Hairdresser	Corner with Downsway
Corner House	Restaurant	Corner with Downsway
P.M.Clack	Builders Merchant	Tiger Timber
Beckley Off-Licence	Wines & Spirits	1 Beckley Parade
Beckley Rabbitry	Bucks at Stud	1 Beckley Parade
H G Boddy	Hairdresser	3 The Parade
G A Okines	Secondhand Furniture	5 The Parade
Bookham Saloons	Transport Services	unknown
D Brookes	Garagiste	Beckley Garage
L F Hancock	Radio & Cycles	unknown

Co-op Hall		between Merityre and Hylands
Co-op Shop		2 New Parade, Merityre
Gau & Lawes	Motor Engineers	Hylands Garage
W.G.Hillier	Market Gardener	Glenthorpe
M Lewis	Dental Surgeon	Bronwen
Arthur Ling	Grocer & Post Office	unknown
G W Gell	Jobbing Gardener	Guildown
K Gell	Dressmaker	Guildown
F Ramsey	Insurance Agent	Petals

GUILDFORD ROAD

Name	Nature of Business	Location
Silas Bedford	Refreshments	unknown
Mrs P. Short	Cliff Tea House	unknown
T W Hammond	Motor Engineer	unknown
Runmore Ltd	Motor Garage	Dagenham Motors
A J Waits	Post Office & Grocer	The Taz Restaurant

LOWER ROAD

Name	Nature of Business	Location
Anchor		Public House 161, Anchor Public House
W Armstrong & Sons	Motor Engineers	242, Whites/Ken Barrington
T R Clark	Stationer	unknown
B L Hamilton	Midwife	Draycott
P Hamshar	Blacksmith	314, Childs
W Harvey	Architect	Dallings
B Rumgary	Pianoforte Lessons	The Little House
A M Easton	Surgeon	Roadside Cottage

LITTLE BOOKHAM STREET

Name	Nature of Business	Location
The Windsor Castle	Public House	Ye Olde Windsor Castle

J Fitzgerald	Boot Repairer	109
A G Sayer	Baker	Paws & Claws until 2000
Howard Weale	Post Office & General store	Howard Weale, General Store
Atlas Works, Burney & Blackburne Ltd	Mechanical Engineering	The Blackburn flats

DORKING ROAD

Name	Nature of Business	Location
George Brine	Livery & Hunting Stables	Kenilworth Stables
W Lawrence	Dairy	unknown
S M Roberts	Phoenice Farm	Phoenice Farm
J Gray	Goldstone Farm	Goldstone Farm
H Brackenbury & Son	Decorator	Paddock Bungalow

EASTWICK ROAD

Name	Nature of Business	Location
Walter Finch	Carman	The Homestead

CRABTREE LANE

Name	Nature of Business	Location
F Casselden	Shoe Repairs	22, Casselden's Shoes
J Casselden	Builder	Englewood

CHILDS HALL ROAD

Name	Nature of Business	Location
A Connisbee	Veterinary Surgeon	unknown
C W Howard	Veterinary Surgeon	unknown

APPENDIX B

LOCAL ENEMY ACTION

TONY PAGE DIARY EXTRACTS

Selected extracts from a diary kept by Tony Page aged 15 yrs and living in Halfway House, Bookham.

30th August 1940　　Began 11.20am　　Ended 12.35pm

We were playing golf at Tyrrell's Wood and were finishing the 9th when the sirens went. They were worse than any cat's chorus. After wondering whether to go on, we walked round to a copse at the 12th tee, hearing a distant hub-bub. This increased and it was obvious that there was a fierce battle in progress over Mickleham and Dorking way and it was approaching. We lay down in the copse. Daddy, looking out, saw 3 Hun over-head and saw the earth from two bombs thrown up in a column 100 feet high x 30 feet wide. We all lay flat and lots more explosions occurred. They were loud 'bangs', not deep muffled explosions. All the time we heard M/G fire and the roar of engines. The noise was amazing and frightening. The sounds of battle receded and after some 25 minutes we ran back to the club house before the all-clear. I heard at least two delayed action bombs come down. The nearest bombs to us were 400 yards away. Seven people were killed. About 40 bombs were dropped.

4th September 1940 Began 1.10pm　　Ended 1.50pm

We heard the roar of many machines coming from Guildford way. Then a fight took place over us and Effingham. There was the usual roaring and noise and we heard M/G fire. One machine came down at Waterloo Farm (Ockham Road North, West Horsley), passing over Uncle Cecil's in flames. Another came down on Netley Heath. Five were brought down altogether. Two bullets hit Uncle Cecil's house. Vickers was hit. 47 killed, 200 injured.

[Extract from 'Wings over Brooklands' pub. 1981: attacked by 20 to 30 Me.110s – 83 died, 419 injured. 15 German aircraft destroyed]

5th September1940 Began 10.35pm　　Ended 5.00am

Aeroplanes buzzed around and two duds were dropped in Fetcham.

6th September 1940 Began 8.50am　　Ended 10.00am

Some Hun passed over us and were heavily shelled; much noise, no dog fights. 14 to 16 Hun passed over in a line from Bookham station to the High Street.

7th September 1940

Leatherhead Golf Club had suffered in a recent raid so we went to have a look at it. There was a very large crater right in front of the club-house, pulling down all the front of the house.

13th September 1940   Began 10.40am

We heard a Hun above the clouds and as we went to the shelter we heard the whistle of falling bombs. I did not hear any explosions but they were very light bombs.

18 fell in Bookham in a straight line from Gau & Lawes to just north of Groveside.

1 blew out the front of the Beckley Pub.

1 on the pavement there.

1 burst a water-main nr. Victoria.

Several at the corner (nr recreation Ground).

1 in dip of road past Victoria in the ditch.

2 in the field opposite Groveside.

About 4 people slightly injured.

18th September 1940   Began 10.05pm

4 bombs were dropped near Polesden Lacey. The explosives were in quick succession and were preceded by a rushing sound as if an aeroplane was coming down low. The bombs fell near the Canadians.

(Note: There were Canadians based at High Barn but not at Polesden House according to Tony and Jessica Page. The bomb map shows about 4/5 bombs and a cluster of incendiaries dropped in Big High Grove halfway between Polesden House and High Barn – RM.)

7th January 1941

The Unexploded Bomb

Landed on the 29th September 1940. Blown up by RE's on 7th January 1941.

About 10ft. long

Weighed 3000 lbs.

Buried about 40ft. down.

There was quite a commotion this afternoon as the time drew near for the event. I had been told about it earlier and was waiting for it to happen, standing on the bridge near the Effingham end of the railway line. A couple of Army lorries with red mudguards and BDS. on the windscreen were

102

pottering around. Trains were stopped on both lines. During all this there was intermittent gunfire. Suddenly, the 'all-clear' began to sound. Just as our own siren was finishing (and it was particularly loud being only 300yds. away), a tall column of purplish dust and smoke shot up from where the bomb was. It was about 200ft. high and 30ft. wide. Simultaneously, there was a deep 'thuroomp'. I ducked under the parapet and suddenly there was an enormously loud bang or report. I jumped on my bike and rushed off to the site. I was about the fifth to arrive there, apart from the RE's. Of the hole nothing was there. There was a ring of earth all round it about 15ft. out and 10ft. high. The earth was mostly in large chunks. In the very centre a large tree which had been some 15ft. away had been deposited and because of the frozen nature of the soil all the soil for 10ft. around the base of the tree had come within a solid mass. I asked one of the men how large it was and he said 3000 lbs. On being asked if it was greater than the one dropped near St. Paul's he said it was as big, if not bigger and therefore certainly one of the biggest, if not the biggest, yet dropped in Great Britain to date.

4th February 1941

Up till now some 70 to 100 HE bombs have fallen in Bookham. No-one has been killed. A few of the more notable occasions have been noted and also some of the larger bombs. Some 300 incendiaries have fallen, including an oil bomb.

19 light bombs. The first to fall. Little damage; straight line from Beckley Pub to Groveside.

A heavy UXB – Bookham Common. Still there.

Lodge at Southey Hall. Also one heavy in grounds near Park View.

Opposite telephone exchange in Church Road.

UXB's up past Hale Pit Road. Narrow escape of Air Raid Warden.

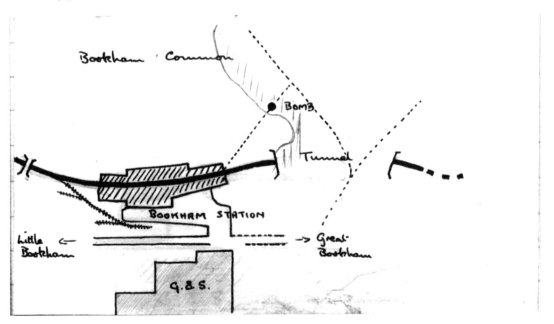

The nearest to us has been some 300yds. away up Lower Road. It was a very light bomb.

Leatherhead has suffered slightly but not too noticeably. One has fallen near the Red Hotel on the gas showrooms. Another, the only one to do serious damage, fell on the oil tanks by the water works near the River Mole. Several fell on Tyrrell's Wood, including some after the blitzkrieg in August/September. There have been slight casualties.

5th May 1941

Whilst bicycling on Bookham Common I thought I would take a look at the site of an unexploded bomb I saw in the Christmas holidays when they were playing around with the one by the station, for by now I fully expected they would have removed it. However, when I got there they were there digging. They had just uncovered it that day and I went and stood over the hole to try and see it; it was not clearly discernible so I made up my mind to come back the next day. The REs told me they were bringing it up some time that week.

6th May 1941

Accordingly, I turned up in the morning to see how things were progressing. This time they allowed me down some 10 feet of the hole, or a side hole which was one of their first attempts. Down at the bottom of a 42 foot hole in the slimy, dripping clay, there lay in one corner a large shining object, the rest of it being concealed under the earth. This was the bomb, and some bomb. The fins had been recovered long ago; they had as usual come off on the way through the earth.

The bomb had fallen sometime last autumn but the men, after digging on it for a short time in January, left it and came back later on. I suppose during April. The bomb was estimated to be about 4000 lbs. in weight. Bigger ones up to 6000 lbs. have apparently been dropped. They were intending to haul this one up the hole (a dangerous business as the least jar would make it go off) and then defuse it. As I was going back to Stowe that day, I had no further opportunity for watching or hearing what happened.

Weight..........4000 lbs.

Size..............10ft. x 2ft. 6in diameter (approx)

Depth............42ft.

Incidentally, it had fallen scarcely 10yds from a small cottage; it had entered the ground by the front gate and lay halfway between there and the road.

June to December 1941

No air raids

25th August 1942

Whilst I was at East Horsley there was a short day alert. I heard the sirens in the distance and Bookham received a warning. Nothing happenend. No further alerts in August.

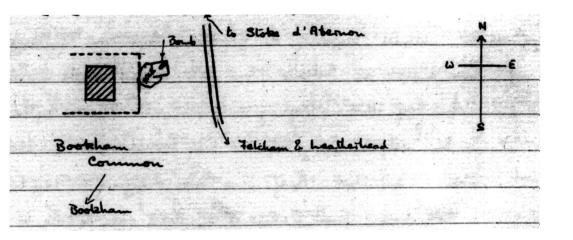

to Stoke d'Abernon

Bomb

Fetcham & Leatherhead

Bookham
Common

Bookham

N
W — E
S

Appendix C

Memories of Turville Kille Jnr

On the day when war was declared I remember playing outside the gate at Downsview and then going inside just after 11am to be told by my mother that we were at war with Germany.

On Friday 13 September 1940 I was coming home from school to be told by a road sweeper in front of Fairfield Cottages, the Council houses, that the Barber's shop (now the fish and chip shop) had been hit by a bomb. Being as this was next door to Downs View I ran as fast as my legs could carry me home.

The bomb had hit the front of the Barber's shop operated by Mr MacDonald. There were customers in the shop , an elderly gentleman and a young lad. Nobody was injured. The raid occurred at about 11am and there was no air raid warning sounded.

Later in the afternoon I remember helping to carry all the MacDonald's china and glasses into our house

When my parents heard the bombs whistling down, my father ducked under a bench in his shed and my mother under the kitchen table.

The bomber dropped 19 bombs straddling the Leatherhead Road from the Barber's shop to the Paddocks. No other damage was done. The police were intrigued that there was only an odd number of bombs dropped.

The whole of the Barber's house as well as the middle shop which was part of the Off-License next door were demolished.

Later on an Air Raid Shelter was built at the front of the site and then sleeping quarters were built just behind the shelter for the firemen who were on duty at night to be ready to man the fire tender which was kept at Gau and Lawes Garage on the corner of Leatherhead and Eastwick Roads.

I remember a bomb being dropped at the southwest corner of Downsway and Blackthorn Roads. There was a wooden garage there with a car inside which was upturned by the blast of the bomb and remained like that until at least the end of the war.

On another occasion I remember my father saying that night he had been up on the Downs putting out incendiary bombs and that the Downs were lit up like Fairyland.

One morning in the summer of 1944 I was on the bus going to school in Leatherhead when a flying bomb or Doodlebug came over. The bus stopped and we all watched it until it came down in a field near Cobham and exploded.

For the last six weeks of the Summer Term at Dorking County Grammar School we spent the whole time in the school air raid shelters. One day being somewhat fed up I climbed up the ladder of the emergency exit and was watching a flying bomb go over until I received a cuff round the head by the teacher in charge and told to get back down the shelter.

These are my main memories of the war.

APPENDIX D

BOOKHAM RESIDENT CASUALTIES

The following table summarises the appearance of the names of Bookham resident casualties on the communal war memorial in St Nicolas churchyard.

	Bookham Memorial Only	Memorial Elsewhere Only	Memorial at both Locations	No Memorial	Subtotal
ACTIVE SERVICE	6	6	4	2	18
HOME DEFENCE	1	0	0	0	1
POLICE	1	0	0	0	1
CIVILIAN	0	0	0	1	1
SUB-TOTAL	8	6	4	3	21

Pilot Officer Frederick Clifford ASHLEY, 21 Sqdn Royal Air Force Volunteer Reserve. Son of Harry Harold and Dorothy May Ashley of Bookham. Died in Ma a on 04/02/1942 aged 21, memorial in Ma a, name on Bookham war memorial.

Lance Corporal Arthur Herbert AYRES, 1st Bn. The Queen's Royal Regiment (West Surrey). Son of Arthur Ayres and of Ellen Sybil Ayres of Great Bookham. Killed in action in Burma on 02/12/1943 aged 24, memorial in Rangoon and on family headstone in St Nicolas churchyard. Name on Bookham war memorial.

Flight Lt Wilfred Guy BALDWIN, Royal Australian Air Force. Son of Ernest James (deceased) and Bessie Baldwin. Died on 20/01/44 aged 35, memorial in St Nicolas churchyard.

Second Lt Malcolm Charles Hugh CANDY, 1/7th Bn The Queen's Royal Regiment (West Surrey). Son of George Spence Candy and Jessie Candy of Bookham. Died in Belgium on 19/05/1940 aged 26, memorial at Heverlee War Cemetery and on the side of the family grave in St Nicolas churchyard. Name on Bookham war memorial. The Dorking Advertiser carried the following article shortly afterwards.

'KILLED IN ACTION.- Much sympathy has been extended to Mrs Candy of White Heather, Lower-road, Great Bookham, in the great loss she has sustained by the death of her only son, 2nd Lieut. Malcolm Hugh Charles Candy of The Queen's Royal Regiment, who has been killed in action. Mr Candy, who was killed on his 26th birthday was a son of the late Dr Spence Candy, who prior to his death some few years ago was in practice in the Bookhams between 15 and 20 years. Before the war Mr Candy held a position in the Sun Insurance Office and was a member of the Honourable Artillery Company. He was called up at the beginning of hostilities. He was educated at Southey Hall School, Great Bookham, and Bradfield. He was a keen sportsman, playing cricket and rugby and being a skilful boxer. A few years ago he took a great interest in the Bookham Boys' Club, where he taught the lads boxing. He was unmarried. Since the outbreak of war, Mrs Spence has been an active worker in connection with the canteen service for evacuated children which has been established in Bookham.'

Bookham War Memorial at St Nicolas Church

Leading Aircraftman Edward Godfrey CARTER, Royal Air Force Volunteer Reserve. Son of John James Carter and Lydia Clara Carter of Little Bookham. Died in Canada on 05/11/1943 aged 19, memorial in Toronto (Prospect) Cemetery. Name on Bookham war memorial.

Lance Corporal Oswald Frederick CREPIN, Queen's Own Royal West Kent Regiment. Died on 16/12/1946 aged 29, Commonwealth War Graves Commission headstone in St Nicolas churchyard.

Pilot Officer John Charles CUNNINGHAM, 50 Sqdn. Royal Air Force Volunteer Reserve. Son of Sir Charles Banks Cunningham, CSI, and of Lady Cunningham (née Macnish) of Flushing House, Church Road, Great Bookham. Flushing House still exists and is on the raised ground opposite the end of Barn Meadow Lane (see 1934 map). Died on 30/05/1941 aged 24. He was the pilot of Hampden I AD867VN undergoing an Air Test It stalled while turning and crashed some 50 yards from Hale Hill Farm, between Hatfield and Hatfield Woodhouse, 2 miles NW of Lindholme, where his squadron was stationed at the time. Memorial in St Nicolas churchyard in the style of a gothic

cross states 'In proud memory…………killed on active service', and also commemorates the subsequent death of his father. Name on Bookham war memorial.

Flight Lt Ernest Frances DEALING, MC, MM, Royal Air Force. Died on 14/11/1946, aged 63, Commonwealth War Graves Commission headstone in St Nicolas churchyard. Whether his death resulted from WW II is perhaps open to question but the CWGC headstone tends to suggest that it did so. However his name does not appear on the Bookham war memorial.

Stanley James GOUGH, Home Guard. Died on 20/04/1941 aged 34, memorial inscription on side of family grave in St Nicolas churchyard.

Major Herbert HILL, Royal Hampshire Regiment. Died on 19/09/1948, aged 55, memorial in St Nicolas churchyard, inscription: 'In proud memory…died through his war service'.

Wing Cdr Peter Andrew KLEBOE, DSO, DFC, AFC, 21 Sqdn Royal Air Force Volunteer Reserve. One of nine siblings, son of Charles Ernest and Maud Martha Kleboe of 'The Croft', Church Road, Great Bookham. 'The Croft' is the first house beyond the first parade of shops on the right hand side of Church Road going towards the station. Died on 21/03/1945 aged 28 on Operation

Carthage, whose target was the Gestapo's Copenhagen HQ. Kleboe's Mosquito dropped to deck level to begin the bomb run, but the tail of the aircraft clipped a 130 foot lighting pylon causing the Mosquito to smash into nearby garages and its bombs to fall in Sonder Boulevard. Memorial in Copenhagen (Bispebjerg) Cemetery and inscription 'killed in action' on Kleboe family headstone in St Nicolas churchyard, and name on Bookham war memorial.

Sgt Dennis Gordon LONGHURST, Royal Air Force Volunteer Reserve. Died on 02/08/1945, presumably in Israel, memorial at Ramleh War Cemetery and name on Bookham war memorial.

Driver Charles Adolphus MOORE, Royal Army Service Corps, son of Adolphus and Esther Moore, husband of Mary Rebecca Lewer Moore of Great Bookham. Died on 29/05/1943 aged 46, Commonwealth War Graves Commission headstone in St Nicolas churchyard, and name on Bookham war memorial.

Gunner Edward Arthur OVENS, 139 Field Regt. Royal Artillery, son of Edward C. T. Ovens and May Ovens of Great Bookham. Died in Burma on 06/02/1944 aged 21, memorial at Taukkyan War Cemetery, and name on Bookham war memorial.

D.POPE: Name on Bookham war memorial but no further information available.

Able Seaman Ronald Charles RANGER, Royal Navy. Died on 17/12/1940, age not recorded. Lost with his A Class destroyer HMS Acheron sunk by a mine off the Isle of Wight with the loss of 196 lives. Death recorded on Portsmouth Naval Memorial and on the family memorial in St Nicolas churchyard with Ernest, who died 01/07/45 aged 64 and Edith Annie who died 12/01/54 aged 71. Name on Bookham war memorial.

John SIMMS: Died 30/08/1940 aged 14 at Reigate Road, Leatherhead when a fleeing German bomber dropped its remaining bombs. He lived at 2 East Street, Great Bookham and was the son of Alfred Simms and buried with presumably, his mother Isabella, who died in 1963. Death recorded at St Nicolas church, but no memorial.

Petty Officer (Radio Mechanic) Gordon Henry STEPHENS RN. Son of William George and Elizabeth Mary Stephens of Great Bookham. Died on 22/08/1944 aged 21 in the Barents Sea when his Ruler Class Escort Carrier, HMS Nabob was struck by an acoustic torpedo fired by U-354 which critically damaged her. Eventually under her own steam she was able to make Scapa Flow for emergency repairs and then dry dock at Rosyth where the remains of 14 of her dead were removed. Memorial at Dunfermline (Douglas Bank) Cemetery.

Flight Lt Douglas Pollock TOUGH 105 Sqdn., RAF Volunteer Reserve. Died on 19/03/1945, place and age not recorded, memorial at Runnymede.

A.J.WHITE. Name on Bookham war memorial but no further information available.

Wilfred (or William) Victor WINFIELD, Police War Reserve. Husband of Lydia Ann Winfield of Newlyn, Dowlans Road, Great Bookham. Died on 28/02/1945 aged 45 from an illness contracted while on war duties, memorial in St Nicolas churchyard, commemorating also the subsequent death of his wife.

Index